BESTIARY

BESTIARY

*An Anthology of Poems
about Animals*

Edited by
Stephen Mitchell

Frog, Ltd.
Berkeley, California

Bestiary: An Anthology of Poems about Animals

Published by Frog, Ltd.

Frog, Ltd. books are distributed by
North Atlantic Books
P.O. Box 12327
Berkeley, California 94712

Distributed to the book trade by Publishers Group West

Cover art: "Tiger" by Mu-ch'i (b. early 13th Century, active 1269).
One of a pair of hanging scrolls, ink with accents in light red on silk,
147 X 93.5 cm. Courtesy of Daitokuji, Kyoto, Japan.

Cover and book design by Paula Morrison

(Continued on page 228, which constitutes an extension of the copyright page)

Library of Congress Cataloging-in-Publication Data

Bestiary : an anthology of poems about animals / edited by Stephen
Mitchell.
     p. cm.
   Includes bibliographical references.
   ISBN 1-883319-48-X
   1. Animals—Poetry. 2. Poetry—Collections. I. Mitchell,
Stephen, 1943 –
PN6110.A7B474 1996
808.81'936—dc20   96-33990
                                   CIP

1 2 3 4 5 6 7 8 9 / 00 99 98 97 96

BY STEPHEN MITCHELL

Poetry
Parables and Portraits

Prose
The Gospel According to Jesus

Translations and Adaptations
Genesis: A New Translation of the Classic Biblical Stories
Ahead of All Parting: The Selected Poetry and Prose of Rainer Maria Rilke
A Book of Psalms
The Selected Poetry of Dan Pagis
Tao Te Ching
The Book of Job
The Selected Poetry of Yehuda Amichai (with Chana Bloch)
The Sonnets to Orpheus
The Lay of the Love and Death of Cornet Christoph Rilke
Letters to a Young Poet
The Notebooks of Malte Laurids Brigge
The Selected Poetry of Rainer Maria Rilke

Edited by Stephen Mitchell
Bestiary: An Anthology of Poems about Animals
Song of Myself
Into the Garden: A Wedding Anthology (with Robert Hass)
The Enlightened Mind: An Anthology of Sacred Prose
The Enlightened Heart: An Anthology of Sacred Poetry
Dropping Ashes on the Buddha: The Teaching of Zen Master Seung Sahn

For Children
The Creation (with paintings by Ori Sherman)

Books on Tape
Genesis
Duino Elegies and The Sonnets to Orpheus
The Gospel According to Jesus
The Enlightened Mind
The Enlightened Heart
Letters to a Young Poet
Parables and Portraits
Tao Te Ching
The Book of Job
Selected Poems of Rainer Maria Rilke

To Jane Hirshfield

CONTENTS

Animals are a form of ourselves. "Primitive" cultures have always known this, and so have poets. If we look at animals from the point of view of the human ego, we may be tempted to consider them as inferior beings, whom we may exploit or extinguish as we wish. But if we see them as they are, we can understand how deeply they embody the intelligence and beauty of the universe.

The more at home we are on this planet, the more respect we naturally feel for all its creatures. "Heaven is my father and earth is my mother," said the eleventh-century Chinese philosopher Chang Tsai, "and even such a small being as I finds an intimate place in their midst. Therefore, what fills the universe I look upon as my body, and what directs the universe I look upon as my nature. All creatures are my brothers and sisters; all things are my companions."

In *Bestiary* I have collected animal poems from many ages and many cultures. My main requirement, besides quality, has been that a poet see the animal with a clear mind—not as a metaphor or symbol, but as it is in itself—and write from a place of deep empathy, entering the animal and, to a greater or lesser extent, becoming one with it. As Basho says,

> Go to the pine if you want to learn about the pine, or to the bamboo if you want if you want to learn about the bamboo. And in doing so, you must let go of your subjective preoccupation with yourself. Otherwise you impose yourself on the object and don't learn. Your poetry arises by itself when you and the object have become one, when you have plunged deep enough into the object to see something like a hidden light glimmering there. However well phrased your poetry may be, if your feeling isn't natural—if you and the object are separate—then your poetry isn't true poetry but merely your subjective counterfeit.

In the following pages there are many poems that have arisen from complete empathy with the consciousness of an animal. Who can read Goethe's astonishing "Death of a Fly," for example, and ever see a fly with quite as much annoyance again?

Bestiary includes excerpts from ancient masterpieces like "The Hymn to the Sun" by Pharaoh Amen-hotep IV, *The Book of Job,* and *The Book of Psalms;* haiku by Basho, Buson, and Issa; poems by Milton and Smart, Blake and Burns, Whitman and Emily Dickinson, Hardy and Hopkins. And since the animal poem attains its full richness and depth in the twentieth century, I have included extensive selections from its greatest modern masters, Rilke, D. H. Lawrence, Marianne Moore, Ponge, and Neruda, as well as poems by other modern poets such as Yeats, Frost, William Carlos Williams, Jeffers, Elizabeth Bishop, and James Wright.

This is a book of passionate and humorous encounters with the vibrant world of the animal. It is also a book about loving the earth. In our time, when selfishness and greed have placed this whole planet on the endangered species list, we particularly need the vision of our great poets. When we read them, we learn that every creature on earth is a treasure and a delight to the heart that contemplates it with undivided attention.

BESTIARY

from THE HYMN TO THE SUN

You appear on the horizon, glorious
sun, begetter of life.
When you rise in the eastern sky,
you fill the whole world with your beauty.
Though you are far away,
you send your light to the earth;
though you shine on men's faces,
your pathways cannot be seen.
You graciously appear, and the darkness
vanishes, and all beings rejoice,
and you shine out to the limits
of everything that you made.
Men wake and stand on their feet,
they wash and put on their clothing
and lift up their arms to thank you,
then go out to their day of work.
Cattle browse in the pastures,
trees and grasses flourish,
geese flutter in the marshes
and stretch out their wings to the sky
in adoration of you,
sheep dance on their hooves,

birds fly into the air
and rejoice that you shine upon them,
fish in the river leap up
before you, and your rays plunge
into the great green sea.
Creator of the seed in women,
you care for the unborn child,
you soothe him so he doesn't cry,
you nurse him even in the womb,
you bring him into the air,
you open his mouth and give him
everything that he needs.
When the chick cries through the eggshell,
you send him the breath of life
and bring his form to completion;
he pecks his way out and stands up
chirping with all his might
and walks on his two feet.

How manifold is your creation,
O one and only God!
How beautiful is this world
created as your heart desired it
when you were all alone!
How beautiful is this world,
with its millions of living creatures—
all people, all animals and plants,
whoever walks on the earth
or flies in the heavens above it.

Do you hunt game for the lioness
    and feed her ravenous cubs,
when they crouch in their den, impatient,
    or lie in ambush in the thicket?
Who finds her prey at nightfall,
    when her cubs are aching with hunger?

Do you tell the antelope to calve
    or ease her when she is in labor?
Do you count the months of her fullness
    and know when her time has come?
She kneels; she tightens her womb;
    she pants, she presses, gives birth.
Her little ones grow up;
    they leave and never return.

Who unties the wild ass
    and lets him wander at will?
He ranges the open prairie
    and roams across the saltlands.
He is far from the tumult of cities;
    he laughs at the driver's whip.
He scours the hills for food,
    in search of anything green.

Is the wild ox willing to serve you?
    Will he spend the night in your stable?
Can you tie a rope to his neck?
    Will he harrow the fields behind you?
Will you trust him because he is powerful
    and leave him to do your work?
Will you wait for him to come back,
    bringing your grain to the barn?

Do you deck the ostrich with wings,
    with elegant plumes and feathers?
She lays her eggs in the dirt
    and lets them hatch on the ground,
forgetting that a foot may crush them
    or sharp teeth crack them open.
She treats her children cruelly,
    as if they were not her own.
For God deprived her of wisdom
    and left her with little sense.
When she spreads her wings to run,
    she laughs at the horse and rider.

Do you give the horse his strength?
    Do you clothe his neck with terror?
Do you make him leap like a locust,
    snort like a blast of thunder?
He paws and champs at the bit;
    he exults as he charges into battle.
He laughs at the sight of danger;
    he does not wince from the sword
or the arrows nipping at his ears
    or the flash of spear and javelin.
With his hooves he swallows the ground;
    he quivers at the sound of the trumpet.

When the trumpet calls, he says "Ah!"
    From far off he smells the battle,
    the thunder of the captains and the shouting.

Do you show the hawk how to fly,
    stretching his wings on the wind?
Do you teach the vulture to soar
    and build his nest in the clouds?
He makes his home on the mountaintop,
    on the unapproachable crag.
He sits and scans for prey;
    from far off his eyes can spot it;
his little ones drink its blood.
    Where the unburied are, he is.

PSALM 104

Unnamable God, you are fathomless;
   I praise you with endless awe.
You are wrapped in light like a cloak;
   you stretch out the sky like a curtain.
You make the clouds your chariot;
   you walk on the wings of the wind.
You use the winds as your messengers,
   thunder and lightning as your servants.
You look at the earth—it trembles;
   you touch the hills and they smoke.
You laid the earth's foundations
   so that they would never be destroyed.
You covered the land with ocean;
   the waters rose higher than the mountains.
They fled at the sound of your voice;
   you thundered and they ran away.
They rushed down into the valleys,
   to the place you appointed for them.
You bounded them, so that they would never
   return to inundate the earth.
You send streams into the valleys,
   and they flow among the hills.

All the animals drink from them;
    the wild asses quench their thirst.
Beside them the birds of the sky dwell,
    singing among the branches.
You water the hills from the sky;
    by your care the whole earth is nourished.
You make grass grow for the cattle
    and grains for the service of mankind,
to bring forth food from the earth
    and bread that strengthens the body,
oil that makes the face shine
    and wine that gladdens the heart.
You plant the trees that grow tall,
    pines, and cedars of Lebanon,
in which many birds build their nests,
    and the stork on the topmost branches.
The mountains are for the wild goats;
    the cliffs are a shelter for the rock squirrels.
You created the moon to count months;
    the sun knows when it must set.
You make darkness, it is night,
    the forest animals emerge.
The young lions roar for their prey,
    seeking their food from God.
The sun rises, they withdraw,
    and lie down in their dens.
Man goes out to his labor
    and works until it is evening.
How infinite are your creatures, Unnamable One!
    With wisdom you made them all.
    The whole earth is filled with your riches.
There is the sea in its vastness,
    where innumerable creatures live,
    fish both tiny and huge.

There sharks swim, and the whale
    that you created to play with.
All these depend on you
    to give them food in due time.
You open your hands—they gather it;
    you give it—they are filled with gladness.
You hide your face—they are stricken;
    you take away their breath—they die
    and return their bodies to the dust.
You send forth your breath—they are born,
    and with them you replenish the earth.
Your glory will last forever;
    eternally you rejoice in your works.
I will sing to you at every moment;
    I will praise you with every breath.
How sweet it is to trust you;
    what joy to embrace your will.
May all selfishness disappear from me,
    and may you always shine from my heart.

CHU CHEN-PO
(9TH CENTURY)

HEDGEHOG

He ambles along like a walking pin-cushion,
Stops and curls up like a chestnut burr.
He's not worried because he's so little.
Nobody is going to slap him around.

Translated by Kenneth Rexroth

from PARADISE LOST

"And God said, 'Let the waters generate
Reptile with spawn abundant, living soul;
And let fowl fly above the earth, with wings
Displayed on the open firmament of heaven.'
And God created the great whales, and each
Soul living, each that crept, which plenteously
The waters generated by their kinds,
And every bird of wing after its kind;
And saw that it was good, and blessed them, saying,
'Be fruitful, multiply, and in the seas
And lakes and running streams the waters fill;
And let the fowl be multiplied on the earth.'
Forthwith the sounds and seas, each creek and bay
With fry innumerable swarm, and shoals
Of fish that with their fins and shining scales
Glide under the green wave in schools that oft
Bank the mid-sea; part, single or with mate,
Graze the sea-weed, their pasture, and through groves
Of coral stray, or sporting with quick glance
Show to the sun their waved coats dropped with gold,
Or in their pearly shells at ease, attend
Moist nutriment, or under rocks their food
In jointed armour watch; on smooth the seal   *smooth: i.e., the sea*

And bended dolphins play, part, huge of bulk,
Wallowing unwieldy, enormous in their gait,
Tempest the ocean; there leviathan,   *the whale*
Hugest of living creatures, on the deep
Stretched like a promontory sleeps or swims,
And seems a moving land, and at his gills
Draws in, and at his trunk spouts out a sea.
Meanwhile the tepid caves, and fens, and shores,
Their brood as numerous hatch, from the egg that soon,
Bursting with kindly rupture, forth disclosed
Their callow young; but feathered soon and fledge,
They summed their pens, and soaring the air sublime   *fully grew their wings*
With clang despised the ground, under a cloud
In prospect; there the eagle and the stork
On cliffs and cedar-tops their eyries build;
Part loosely wing the region; part, more wise,   *separately*
In common, ranged in figure wedge their way,
Intelligent of seasons, and set forth
Their airy caravan, high over seas
Flying, and over lands with mutual wing
Easing their flight; so steers the prudent crane
Her annual voyage, borne on winds; the air
Floats as they pass, fanned with unnumbered plumes;
From branch to branch the smaller birds with song
Solaced the woods, and spread their painted wings,
Till even, nor then the solemn nightingale
Ceased warbling, but all night tuned her soft lays;
Others on silver lakes and rivers bathed
Their downy breast; the swan, with archèd neck
Between her white wings mantling proudly, rows   *wrapping herself as in a cloak*
Her state with oary feet; yet oft they quit
The dank, and rising on stiff pennons, tower
The mid aerial sky; others on ground
Walked firm—the crested cock, whose clarion sounds

The silent hours, and the other, whose gay train
Adorns him, coloured with the florid hue
Of rainbows and starry eyes. The waters thus
With fish replenished, and the air with fowl,
Evening and morning solemnized the fifth day.
  "The sixth, and of Creation last, arose
With evening harps and matin, when God said,
'Let the earth bring forth soul living in her kind,
Cattle and creeping things, and beast of the earth,
Each in their kind.' The earth obeyed, and straight
Opening her fertile womb, teemed at a birth
Innumerous living creatures, perfect forms,
Limbed and full grown. Out of the ground uprose
As from his lair the wild beast, where he wons   *dwells*
In forest wild, in thicket, brake, or den;
Among the trees in pairs they rose, they walked;
The cattle in the fields and meadows green:
Those rare and solitary, these in flocks
Pasturing at once, and in broad herds upsprung.
The grassy clods now calved, now half appeared
The tawny lion, pawing to get free
His hinder parts, then springs, as broke from bonds,
And rampant shakes his brinded mane; the ounce,   *rearing; streaked; lynx*
The libbard, and the tiger, as the mole   *leopard*
Rising, the crumbled earth above them threw
In hillocks; the swift stag from under ground
Bore up his branching head; scarce from his mould
Behemoth, biggest born of earth, upheaved   *the elephant*
His vastness; fleeced the flocks and bleating rose,
As plants; ambiguous between sea and land,
The river-horse and scaly crocodile.   *hippopotamus*
At once came forth whatever creeps the ground,
Insect or worm; those waved their limber fans
For wings, and smallest lineaments exact

In all the liveries decked of summer's pride
With spots of gold and purple, azure and green;
These as a line their long dimension drew
Streaking the ground with sinuous trace; not all
Minims of nature; some of serpent kind,   *tiniest creatures*
Wondrous in length and corpulence, involved   *wound*
Their snaky folds, and added wings. First crept
The parsimonious emmet, provident   *ant*
Of future, in small room large heart enclosed,
Pattern of just equality perhaps
Hereafter, joined in her popular tribes
Of commonalty; swarming next appeared
The female bee, that feeds her husband drone
Deliciously, and builds her waxen cells
With honey stored; the rest are numberless,
And thou their natures know'st, and gav'st them names,   *thou: Adam*
Needless to thee repeated; nor unknown
The serpent, subtlest beast of all the field,
Of huge extent sometimes, with brazen eyes
And hairy mane terrific, though to thee
Not noxious, but obedient at thy call."

BASHO
(1644–1694)

SELECTED HAIKU

Old pond,
frog jumps in—
    splash.

Translated by Michael Katz

On a withered branch
A crow is perched:
    An autumn evening.

Fleas, lice,
A horse pissing
    By my bed.

Wake up! wake up!
Be my friend,
    Sleeping butterfly.

Translated by Robert Aitken

Autumn moonlight—
a worm digs silently
into the chestnut.

The sea darkening—
the wild duck's call
is faintly white.

A bee
staggers out
of the peony.

Clear water—
a tiny crab
crawling up my leg.

Good house:
sparrows out back
feasting in the millet.

Singing, flying, singing,
the cuckoo
keeps busy.

A cicada shell;
it sang itself
  utterly away.

First winter rain—
even the monkey
  seems to want a raincoat.

Dusk
dims the hawk's eyes
  and the quail start chirping.

What voice,
what song, spider,
  in the autumn wind?

Not this human sadness,
cuckoo,
  but your solitary cry.

All day long—
but not long enough for the skylark,
  singing, singing.

Stillness—
the cicada's cry
drills into the rocks.

A caterpillar,
this deep in fall—
still not a butterfly.

The dragonfly
can't quite land
on that blade of grass.

Cold night: the wild duck,
sick, falls from the sky
and sleeps awhile.

Bush warbler:
shits on the rice cakes
on the porch rail.

Still alive
and frozen in one lump—
the sea slugs.

The long rains—
silkworms sick
in the mulberry fields.

Translated by Robert Hass

BUSON
(1715–1783)

SELECTED HAIKU

That snail—
one long horn, one short,
what's on his mind?

How awkward it looks
swimming—
the frog.

Sparrow singing—
its tiny mouth
open.

They end their flight
one by one—
crows in the dusk.

Going home,
the horse stumbles
    in the winter wind.

Butterfly
sleeping
    on the temple bell.

The short night—
on the hairy caterpillar
    beads of dew.

A flying squirrel
chewing on a bird
    in the withered fields.

Evening wind:
water laps
    the heron's legs.

A bat flits
in moonlight
    above the plum blossoms.

Dawn—
fish the cormorants haven't caught
swimming in the shallows.

Sudden shower—
a flock of sparrows
clinging to the grasses.

It cried three times,
the deer,
then silence.

Translated by Robert Hass

from JUBILATE AGNO

For I will consider my Cat Jeoffry.

For he is the servant of the Living God, duly and daily serving him.

For at the first glance of the glory of God in the East he worships in
his way.

For is this done by wreathing his body seven times round with
elegant quickness.

For then he leaps up to catch the musk, which is the blessing of God
upon his prayer.

For he rolls upon prank to work it in.

For having done duty and received blessing he begins to consider
himself.

For this he performs in ten degrees.

For first he looks upon his fore-paws to see if they are clean.

For secondly he kicks up behind to clear away there.

For thirdly he works it upon stretch with the fore paws extended.

For fourthly he sharpens his paws by wood.

For fiftly he washes himself.

For sixthly he rolls upon wash.

For Seventhly he fleas himself, that he may not be interrupted upon
the beat.

For Eightly he rubs himself against a post.

For Ninthly he looks up for his instructions.

For Tenthly he goes in quest of food.

For having consider'd God and himself he will consider his neighbour.

For if he meets another cat he will kiss her in kindness.

For when he takes his prey he plays with it to give it chance.

For one mouse in seven escapes by his dallying.

For when his day's work is done his business more properly begins.

For he keeps the Lord's watch in the night against the adversary.

For he counteracts the powers of darkness by his electrical skin &
glaring eyes.

For he counteracts the Devil, who is death, by brisking about the life.

For in his morning orisons he loves the sun and the sun loves him.

For he is of the tribe of Tiger.

For the Cherub Cat is a term of the Angel Tiger.

For he has the subtlety and hissing of a serpent, which in goodness
he suppresses.

For he will not do destruction, if he is well-fed, neither will he spit
without provocation.

For he purrs in thankfulness, when God tells him he's a good Cat.

For he is an instrument for the children to learn benevolence upon.

For every house is incompleat without him & a blessing is lacking
in the spirit.

For the Lord commanded Moses concerning the cats at the depar-
ture of the Children of Israel from Egypt.

For every family had one cat at least in the bag.

For the English Cats are the best in Europe.

For he is the cleanest in the use of his fore-paws of any quadrupede.

For the dexterity of his defence is an instance of the love of God to
him exceedingly.

For he is the quickest to his mark of any creature.

For he is tenacious of his point.

For he is a mixture of gravity and waggery.

For he knows that God is his Saviour.

For there is nothing sweeter than his peace when at rest.

For there is nothing brisker than his life when in motion.

For he is of the Lord's poor and so indeed is he called by benevo-
lence perpetually—Poor Jeoffry! poor Jeoffry! the rat has bit thy
throat.

For I bless the name of the Lord Jesus that Jeoffry is better.

For the divine spirit comes about his body to sustain it in compleat cat.

For his tongue is exceeding pure so that it has in purity what it wants in musick.

For he is docile and can learn certain things.

For he can set up with gravity which is patience upon approbation.

For he can fetch and carry, which is patience in employment.

For he can jump over a stick which is patience upon proof positive.

For he can spraggle upon waggle at the word of command.

For he can jump from an eminence into his master's bosom.

For he can catch the cork and toss it again.

For he is hated by the hypocrite and miser.

For the former is affraid of detection.

For the latter refuses the charge.

For he camels his back to bear the first notion of business.

For he is good to think on, if a man would express himself neatly.

For he made a great figure in Egypt for his signal services.

For he killed the Icneumon-rat very pernicious by land.

For his ears are so acute that they sting again.

For from this proceeds the passing quickness of his attention.

For by stroaking of him I have found out electricity.

For I perceived God's light about him both wax and fire.

For the Electrical fire is the spiritual substance, which God sends from heaven to sustain the bodies both of man and beast.

For God has blessed him in the variety of his movements.

For, tho he cannot fly, he is an excellent clamberer.

For his motions upon the face of the earth are more than any other quadrupede.

For he can tread to all the measures upon the musick.

For he can swim for life.

For he can creep.

from A SONG TO DAVID

For ADORATION seasons change,
And order, truth, and beauty range,
 Adjust, attract, and fill:
The grass the polyanthus cheques;
And polish'd porphyry reflects,
 By the descending rill.

Rich almonds colour to the prime
For ADORATION; tendrils climb,
 And fruit-trees pledge their gems;
And Ivis* with her gorgeous vest
Builds for her eggs her cunning nest,
 And bell-flowers bow their stems.

With vinous syrup cedars spout;
From rocks pure honey gushing out,
 For ADORATION springs:
All scenes of painting croud the map
Of nature; to the mermaid's pap
 The scaled infant clings.

* Humming-bird.

The spotted ounce and playsome cubs
Run rustling 'mongst the flow'ring shrubs,
    And lizards feed the moss;
For ADORATION beasts* embark,
While waves upholding halcyon's ark
    No longer roar and toss.

While Israel sits beneath his fig,
With coral root and amber sprig
    The wean'd advent'rer sports;
Where to the palm the jasmin cleaves,
For ADORATION 'mong the leaves
    The gale his peace reports.

Increasing days their reign exalt,
Nor in the pink and mottled vault
    Th' opposing spirits tilt;
And, by the coasting reader spy'd,
The silverlings and crusions glide
    For ADORATION gilt.

For ADORATION rip'ning canes
And cocoa's purest milk detains
    The western pilgrim's staff;
Where rain in clasping boughs inclos'd,
And vines with oranges dispos'd,
    Embow'r the social laugh.

Now labour his reward receives,
For ADORATION counts his sheaves
    To peace, her bounteous prince;
The nectarine his strong tint imbibes,

* There is a large quadruped that preys upon fish, and provides himself with a piece of timber for that purpose, with which he is very handy.

And apples of ten thousand tribes,
    And quick peculiar quince.

The wealthy crops of whit'ning rice,
'Mongst thyine woods and groves of spice,
    For ADORATION grow;
And, marshall'd in the fenced land,
The peaches and pomegranates stand,
    Where wild carnations blow.

The laurels with the winter strive;
The crocus burnishes alive
    Upon the snow-clad earth:
For ADORATION myrtles stay
To keep the garden from dismay,
    And bless the sight from dearth.

The pheasant shows his pompous neck;
And ermine, jealous of a speck
    With fear eludes offence:
The sable, with his glossy pride,
For ADORATION is descried,
    Where frosts the wave condense.

The chearful holly, pensive yew,
And holy thorn, their trim renew;
    The squirrel hoards his nuts:
All creatures batten o'er their stores,
And careful nature all her doors
    For ADORATION shuts.

For ADORATION, David's psalms
Lift up the heart to deeds of alms;
    And he, who kneels and chants,
Prevails his passions to controul,

Finds meat and med'cine to the soul,
    Which for translation pants.

For ADORATION, beyond match,
The scholar bulfinch aims to catch
    The soft flute's iv'ry touch;
And, careless on the hazle spray,
The daring redbreast keeps at bay
    The damsel's greedy clutch.

For ADORATION, in the skies,
The Lord's philosopher espies
    The Dog, the Ram, and Rose;
The planets ring, Orion's sword;
Nor is his greatness less ador'd
    In the vile worm that glows.

For ADORATION on the strings*
The western breezes work their wings,
    The captive ear to sooth.—
Hark! 'tis a voice—how still, and small—
That makes the cataracts to fall,
    Or bids the sea be smooth.

For ADORATION, incense comes
From bezoar, and Arabian gums;
    And from the civet's furr.
But as for pray'r, or ere it faints,
Far better is the breath of saints
    Than galbanum and myrrh.

For ADORATION from the down
Of dam'sins to th' anana's crown,

* Æolian harp.

God sends to tempt the taste;
And while the luscious zest invites
The sense, that in the scene delights,
    Commands desire be chaste.

For ADORATION, all the paths
Of grace are open, all the baths
    Of purity refresh;
And all the rays of glory beam
To deck the man of God's esteem,
    Who triumphs o'er the flesh.

For ADORATION, in the dome
Of Christ the sparrows find an home,
    And on his olives perch:
The swallow also dwells with thee,
O man of God's humility,
    Within his Saviour's CHURCH.

Sweet is the dew that falls betimes,
And drops upon the leafy limes;
    Sweet Hermon's fragrant air:
Sweet is the lily's silver bell,
And sweet the wakeful tapers smell
    That watch for early pray'r.

Sweet the young nurse with love intense,
Which smiles o'er sleeping innocence;
    Sweet when the lost arrive:
Sweet the musician's ardour beats,
While his vague mind's in quest of sweets,
    The choicest flow'rs to hive.

Sweeter in all the Strains of love,
The language of thy turtle dove,

Pair'd to thy swelling chord;
Sweeter with ev'ry grace endu'd,
The glory of thy gratitude,
    Respir'd unto the Lord.

Strong is the horse upon his speed;
Strong in pursuit the rapid glede,
    Which makes at once his game:
Strong the tall ostrich on the ground;
Strong through the turbulent profound
    Shoots xiphias* to his aim.

Strong is the lion—like a coal
His eye-ball—like a bastion's mole
    His chest against the foes:
Strong the gier-eagle on his sail,
Strong against tide, th' enormous whale
    Emerges, as he goes.

But stronger still, in earth and air,
And in the sea, the man of pray'r;
    And far beneath the tide;
And in the seat to faith assign'd,
Where ask is have, where seek is find,
    Where knock is open wide.

* Sword-fish.

WILLIAM COWPER
(1731–1800)

THE SNAIL

To grass, or leaf, or fruit, or wall,
The Snail sticks close, nor fears to fall,
As if he grew there, house and all
    Together.

Within that house secure he hides,
When danger imminent betides
Of storm, or other harm besides,
    Of weather.

Give but his horns the slightest touch,
His self-collecting power is such,
He shrinks into his house, with much
    Displeasure.

Where'er he dwells, he dwells alone,
Except himself has chattels none,
Well satisfied to be his own
    Whole treasure.

Thus hermit-like his life he leads,
Nor partner of his banquet needs,
And if he meets one, only feeds
    The faster.

Who seeks him must be worse than blind
(He and his house are so combin'd)
If, finding it, he fails to find
    Its master.

EPITAPH ON A HARE

Here lies, whom hound did ne'er pursue,
　　Nor swifter greyhound follow,
Whose foot ne'er tainted morning dew,
　　Nor ear heard huntsman's hallow,

Old Tiney, surliest of his kind,
　　Who, nursed with tender care,
And to domestic bounds confined,
　　Was still a wild Jack-hare.

Though duly from my hand he took
　　His pittance every night,
He did it with a jealous look,
　　And, when he could, would bite.

His diet was of wheaten bread,
　　And milk, and oats, and straw,
Thistles, or lettuces instead,
　　With sand to scour his maw.

On twigs of hawthorn he regaled,
　　On pippins' russet peel;
And, when his juicy salads failed,
　　Sliced carrots pleased him well.

A Turkey carpet was his lawn,
    Whereon he loved to bound,
To skip and gambol like a fawn,
    And swing his rump around.

His frisking was at evening hours,
    For then he lost his fear;
But most before approaching showers,
    Or when a storm drew near.

Eight years and five round-rolling moons
    He thus saw steal away,
Dozing out all his idle noons,
    And every night at play.

I kept him for his humour' sake,
    For he would oft beguile
My heart of thoughts that made it ache,
    And force me to a smile.

But now, beneath this walnut-shade
    He finds his long, last home,
And waits in snug concealment laid,
    Till gentler Puss shall come.

He, still more agèd, feels the shocks
    From which no care can save,
And, partner once of Tiney's box,
    Must soon partake his grave.

JOHANN WOLFGANG GOETHE
(1749–1832)

DEATH OF A FLY

Without a pause she drinks the treacherous brew,
more powerfully seduced with each sweet sip;
she feels serene, invulnerable, although
her slender legs already have grown stiff,
no longer skilled enough to wash her face
or clean her delicate, translucent wings.
Thus, in delight, life smoothly slips away.
The numbness spreads, she barely feels a thing;
yet on she sips, and even as she does,
death covers with a cloud her thousand eyes.

THE TYGER

Tyger Tyger, burning bright,
In the forests of the night;
What immortal hand or eye,
Could frame thy fearful symmetry?

In what distant deeps or skies,
Burnt the fire of thine eyes?
On what wings dare he aspire?
What the hand dare sieze the fire?

And what shoulder, & what art,
Could twist the sinews of thy heart?
And when thy heart began to beat,
What dread hand? & what dread feet?

What the hammer? what the chain?
In what furnace was thy brain?
What the anvil? what dread grasp
Dare its deadly terrors clasp!

When the stars threw down their spears
And water'd heaven with their tears:
Did he smile his work to see?
Did he who made the Lamb make thee?

Tyger Tyger burning bright,
In the forests of the night:
What immortal hand or eye,
Dare frame thy fearful symmetry?

ROBERT BURNS
(1759–1796)

TO A MOUSE
On turning her up in her nest with the plough,
November 1785

1

Wee, sleekit, cowrin, tim'rous beastie,	*sleek*
O, what a panic's in thy breastie!	
Thou need na start awa sae hasty	
Wi' bickering brattle!	*hurrying scamper*
I wad be laith to rin an' chase thee,	*loth*
Wi' murdering pattle!	*plow staff*

2

I'm truly sorry man's dominion
Has broken Nature's social union,
An' justifies that ill opinion
Which makes thee startle
At me, thy poor, earth-born companion
An' fellow mortal!

3

I doubt na, whyles, but thou may thieve;	*sometimes*
What then? poor beastie, thou maun live!	*must*
A daimen icker in a thrave,	*odd ear in twenty-four sheaves*
'S a sma' request;	
I'll get a blessin wi' the lave,	
An' never miss't!	

4

Thy wee-bit housie, too, in ruin!
Its silly wa's the win's are strewin! *feeble walls*
An' naething, now, to big a new ane, *build; one*
    O' foggage green! *coarse grass*
An' bleak December's win's ensuin,
    Baith snell an' keen! *both bitter*

5

Thou saw the fields laid bare an' waste,
An' weary winter comin fast,
An' cozie here, beneath the blast,
    Thou thought to dwell,
Till crash! the cruel coulter past *plow blade*
    Out thro' thy cell.

6

That wee bit heap o' leaves an' stibble, *stubble*
Has cost thee monie a weary nibble! *many*
Now thou's turned out, for a' thy trouble,
    But house or hald, *without; holding*
To thole the winter's sleety dribble, *endure*
    An' cranreuch cauld! *hoar-frost*

7

But Mousie, thou art no thy lane, *alone*
In proving foresight may be vain:
The best-laid schemes o' mice an' men
    Gang aft agley, *go often askew*
An' lea'e us nought but grief an' pain, *leave*
    For promis'd joy!

8

Still thou art blest, compared wi' me!
The present only toucheth thee:
But och! I backward cast my e'e,
On prospects drear!
An' forward, tho' I canna see,
I guess an' fear!

ISSA
(1763–1827)

SELECTED HAIKU

If the times were good,
I'd ask one more of you to join me,
    flies.

My cat,
frisking in the scale,
    records its weight.

A huge frog and I,
staring at each other,
    neither of us moves.

Climb Mount Fuji,
O snail,
    but slowly, slowly.

Deer licking
first frost
  from each other's coats.

Having slept, the cat gets up,
yawns, goes out
  to make love.

O flea! whatever you do,
don't jump;
  that way is the river.

One human being,
one fly,
  in a large room.

Red morning sky,
snail;
  are you glad of it?

Ah! the evening cuckoo—
listen, you wretched flies
  and other creeping things.

Don't kill that fly!
Look— it's wringing its hands,
　　wringing its feet.

Ｔhe bedbugs
scatter as I clean,
　　parents and children.

Under the evening moon
the snail
　　is stripped to the waist.

Hearing a voice
the doe takes her stand
　　beside the fawn.

Garden butterfly:
baby crawls, it flies,
　　she crawls, it flies.

Spring rain:
a mouse is lapping
　　the Sumida River.

Hell:
    Bright autumn moon—
pond snails crying
    in the saucepan.

    Visiting the graves,
the old dog
    leads the way.

    That wren—
looking here, looking there.
    You lose something?

    I'm going to roll over,
so please move,
    cricket.

    Even with insects—
some can sing,
    some can't.

    The old dog—
listening for the songs
    of earthworms?

Don't worry, spiders,
I keep house
    casually.

The crow
walks along there
    as if it were tilling the field.

Not knowing
it's a tub they're in,
    the fish cooling at the gate.

How *much*
are you enjoying yourself,
    tiger moth?

Insects on a bough,
floating downriver,
    still singing.

The mountain cuckoo—
a fine voice,
    and proud of it!

Flopped on the fan,
the big cat
    sleeping.

Hey, sparrow!
out of the way,
    Horse is coming.

Fleas in my hut,
it's my fault
    you're getting so skinny.

"Come on! the bamboo grove,
then the plum tree"
    —the mother sparrow.

The new foal
sticks her nose up
    through the irises.

No doubt about it,
the mountain cuckoo
    is a crybaby.

With its mother on guard,
the foal laps
    clear water.

Everything's right with the world—
let another fly
    land on the rice bowl.

The first firefly,
then off!
    wind left in my hand.

Cicadas in the pines,
how loud
    for it to be noon?

Toad,
your wife is waiting,
    your children are waiting.

Little sparrow,
want to help me
    pick lice?

The dragonfly,
dressed in red,
off to the festival.

My old home—
the snail's face
is the face of Buddha.

Mosquito at my ear—
does it think
I'm deaf?

I'm going out,
flies, so relax,
make love.

For you fleas too
the nights must be long,
they must be lonely.

The toad! It looks like
it could belch
a cloud.

These sea slugs,
they just don't seem
Japanese.

The cuckoo sings
to me, to the mountain,
    to me, to the mountain.

The snail gets up
and goes to bed
    with very little fuss.

The woodpecker—
still drilling
    as the sun goes down.

Translated by Robert Hass

Even for the emperor
the nightingale sings
    the same song.

Mountains,
reflected
    in the dragonfly's eye.

Tired of walking
along my arm, the flea
jumps.

Hey cat!
hurry up,
your wife is calling.

Where there are humans,
there are flies
and Buddhas.

Look out:
you'll bump your heads
on that stone, fireflies.

The mouse
licks a raindrop
from the bamboo leaf.

In this world
even butterflies
have to earn their living.

The cat looks up,
a grain of rice
   stuck to his nose.

Morning:
the nightingale's song,
   drenched with rain.

Watch over my grave
when I die,
   grasshopper.

The frog squats, safe
in the Buddha's
   stone hand.

Now that you've taken off
your skin, snake,
   are you cooler?

Trusting my shoe,
the butterfly sleeps
   on the ground.

Listen, insects,
listen:
    the bell of transience.

Does the caged
nightingale hear?—
    mountain cuckoo.

Peeking out
from the morning-glories:
    a mouse.

Big horse
scratching his ass on
    the cherry tree.

Right next to my foot:
when did you get here,
    snail?

Even when he shits,
the nightingale
    sings.

Owls are calling
to the fireflies,
  "Come, come."

Flying out from
the Great Buddha's nose:
a swallow.

I'm peeing:
look out,
  grasshopper.

Don't cry, insects:
even lovers, even stars
  must say goodbye.

JOHN CLARE
(1793–1864)

HARES AT PLAY

The birds are gone to bed, the cows are still,
And sheep lie panting on each old mole hill
And underneath the willows' grey-green bough
Like toil a-resting—lies the fallow plough.
The timid hares throw daylight's fears away
On the lane's road to dust and dance and play,
Then dabble in the grain, by nought deterred,
To lick the dewfall from the barley's beard.
Then out they sturt again and round the hill   *move suddenly*
Like happy thoughts—dance—squat—and loiter still
Till milking maidens in the early morn
Jingle their yokes and sturt them in the corn.
Through well-known beaten paths each nimbling hare
Sturts quick as fear—and seeks its hidden lair.

JOHN CLARE

THE MOUSE'S NEST

I found a ball of grass among the hay
And progged it as I passed and went away;   *prodded*
And when I looked I fancied something stirred,
And turned again and hoped to catch the bird—
When out an old mouse bolted in the wheats
With all her young ones hanging at her teats;
She looked so odd and so grotesque to me,
I ran and wondered what the thing could be,
And pushed the knapweed bunches where I stood;
Then the mouse hurried from the craking brood.   *crawling*
The young ones squeaked, and as I went away
She found her nest again among the hay.
The water o'er the pebbles scarce could run
And broad old cesspools glittered in the sun.

TO A WATERFOWL

Whither, midst falling dew,
While glow the heavens with the last steps of day,
Far, through their rosy depths, dost thou pursue
    Thy solitary way?

Vainly the fowler's eye
Might mark thy distant flight to do thee wrong,
As, darkly painted on the crimson sky,
    Thy figure floats along.

Seek'st thou the plashy brink
Of weedy lake, or marge of river wide,
Or where the rocking billows rise and sink
    On the chafed ocean-side?

There is a Power whose care
Teaches thy way along that pathless coast—
The desert and illimitable air—
    Lone wandering, but not lost.

All day thy wings have fanned,
At that far height, the cold, thin atmosphere,
Yet stoop not, weary, to the welcome land,
    Though the dark night is near.

And soon that toil shall end;
Soon shalt thou find a summer home, and rest,
And scream among thy fellows; reeds shall bend,
    Soon, o'er thy sheltered nest.

    Thou'rt gone, the abyss of heaven
Hath swallowed up thy form; yet, on my heart
Deeply has sunk the lesson thou hast given,
    And shall not soon depart.

    He who, from zone to zone,
Guides through the boundless sky thy certain flight,
In the long way that I must tread alone,
    Will lead my steps aright.

from SONG OF MYSELF

I believe a leaf of grass is no less than the journeywork of the stars,
And the pismire is equally perfect, and a grain of sand, and the egg
    of the wren,
And the tree-toad is a chef-d'œuvre for the highest,
And the running blackberry would adorn the parlors of heaven,
And the narrowest hinge in my hand puts to scorn all machinery,
And the cow crunching with depressed head surpasses any statue,
And a mouse is miracle enough to stagger sextillions of infidels.

I find I incorporate gneiss and coal and long-threaded moss and
    fruits and grains and esculent roots,
And am stucco'd with quadrupeds and birds all over,
And have distanced what is behind me for good reasons,
And call any thing close again when I desire it.

In vain the speeding or shyness,
In vain the plutonic rocks send their old heat against my approach,
In vain the mastadon retreats beneath its own powdered bones,
In vain objects stand leagues off and assume manifold shapes,
In vain the ocean setting in hollows and the great monsters lying low,
In vain the buzzard houses herself with the sky,
In vain the snake slides through the creepers and logs,
In vain the elk takes to the inner passes of the woods,

In vain the razorbilled auk sails far north to Labrador,
I follow quickly .... I ascend to the nest in the fissure of the cliff.

I think I could turn and live awhile with the animals .... they are
    so placid and self-contained,
I stand and look at them long and long.

They do not sweat and whine about their condition,
They do not lie awake in the dark and weep for their sins,
They do not make me sick discussing their duty to God,
Not one is dissatisfied .... not one is demented with the mania of
    owning things,
Not one kneels to another nor to his kind that lived thousands of
    years ago,
Not one is respectable or industrious over the whole earth.

So they show their relations to me and I accept them;
They bring me tokens of myself. .... they evince them plainly in
    their possession.

I do not know where they got those tokens,
I must have passed that way untold times ago and negligently
    dropt them,
Myself moving forward then and now and forever,
Gathering and showing more always and with velocity,
Infinite and omnigenous and the like of these among them;
Not too exclusive toward the reachers of my remembrancers,
Picking out here one that I love,
Choosing to go with him on brotherly terms.

A gigantic beauty of a stallion, fresh and responsive to my caresses,
Head high in the forehead and wide between the ears,
Limbs glossy and supple, tail dusting the ground,
Eyes well apart and full of sparkling wickedness .... ears finely cut
    and flexibly moving.

His nostrils dilate .... my heels embrace him .... his well built
    limbs tremble with pleasure .... we speed around and return.
I but use you a moment and then I resign you stallion .... and do
    not need your paces, and outgallop them,
And myself as I stand or sit pass faster than you.

WALT WHITMAN

THE DALLIANCE OF THE EAGLES

Skirting the river road, (my forenoon walk, my rest,)
Skyward in air a sudden muffled sound, the dalliance of the eagles,
The rushing amorous contact high in space together,
The clinching interlocking claws, a living, fierce, gyrating wheel,
Four beating wings, two beaks, a swirling mass tight grappling,
In tumbling turning clustering loops, straight downward falling,
Till o'er the river pois'd, the twain yet one, a moment's lull,
A motionless still balance in the air, then parting, talons loosing,
Upward again on slow-firm pinions slanting, their separate diverse
    flight,
She hers, he his, pursuing.

A Bird came down the Walk—
He did not know I saw—
He bit an Angleworm in halves
And ate the fellow, raw,

And then he drank a Dew
From a convenient Grass—
And then hopped sidewise to the Wall
To let a Beetle pass—

He glanced with rapid eyes
That hurried all around—
They looked like frightened Beads, I thought—
He stirred his Velvet Head

Like one in danger, Cautious,
I offered him a Crumb
And he unrolled his feathers
And rowed him softer home—

Than Oars divide the Ocean,
Too silver for a seam—
Or Butterflies, off Banks of Noon
Leap, plashless as they swim.

She sights a Bird—she chuckles—
She flattens—then she crawls—
She runs without the look of feet—
Her eyes increase to Balls—

Her jaws stir—twitching—hungry—
Her Teeth can hardly stand—
She leaps, but Robin leaped the first—
Ah, Pussy, of the Sand,

The Hopes so juicy ripening —
You almost bathed your Tongue—
When Bliss disclosed a hundred Toes—
And fled with every one—

The Spider holds a Silver Ball
In unperceived Hands—
And dancing softly to Himself
His Yarn of Pearl—unwinds—

He plies from Nought to Nought—
In unsubstantial Trade—
Supplants our Tapestries with His—
In half the period—

An Hour to rear supreme
His Continents of Light—
Then dangle from the Housewife's Broom—
His Boundaries—forgot—

A narrow fellow in the Grass
Occasionally rides—
You may have met Him—did you not
His notice sudden is—

The Grass divides as with a Comb—
A spotted shaft is seen—
And then it closes at your feet
And opens further on—

He likes a Boggy Acre
A Floor too cool for Corn—
Yet when a Boy, and Barefoot—
I more than once at Noon

Have passed, I thought, a Whip lash
Unbraiding in the Sun
When stooping to secure it
It wrinkled, and was gone—

Several of Nature's People
I know, and they know me—
I feel for then a transport
Of cordiality—

But never met this Fellow
Attended, or alone
Without a tighter breathing
And Zero at the Bone—

EMILY DICKINSON

A Route of Evanescence
With a revolving Wheel—
A Resonance of Emerald—
A Rush of Cochineal—
And every Blossom on the Bush
Adjusts its tumbled Head—
The mail from Tunis, probably,
An easy Morning's Ride—

One of the ones that Midas touched
Who failed to touch us all
Was that confiding Prodigal
The reeling Oriole—

So drunk he disavows it
With badinage divine—
So dazzling we mistake him
For an alighting Mine—

A Pleader—a Dissembler—
An Epicure—a Thief—
Betimes an Oratorio—
An Ecstasy in chief—

The Jesuit of Orchards
He cheats as he enchants
Of an entire Attar
For his decamping wants—

The splendor of a Burmah
The Meteor of Birds,
Departing like a Pageant
Of Ballads and of Bards—

I never thought that Jason sought
For any Golden Fleece
But then I am a rural man
With thoughts that make for Peace—

But if there were a Jason,
Tradition bear with me
Behold his lost Aggrandizement
Upon the Apple Tree—

The Bat is dun, with wrinkled wings—
Like fallow Article—
And not a song pervade his Lips—
Or none perceptible.

His small Umbrella quaintly halved
Describing in the Air
An Arc alike inscrutable
Elate Philosopher.

Deputed from what Firmament—
Of what Astute Abode—
Empowered with what Malignity
Auspiciously withheld—

To his adroit Creator
Ascribe no less the praise—
Beneficent, believe me,
His Eccentricities—

THOMAS HARDY

(1840–1928)

THE DARKLING THRUSH

I leant upon a coppice gate
　　When Frost was spectre-gray,
And Winter's dregs made desolate
　　The weakening eye of day.
The tangled bine-stems scored the sky
　　Like strings of broken lyres,
And all mankind that haunted nigh
　　Had sought their household fires.

The land's sharp features seemed to be
　　The Century's corpse outleant,
His crypt the cloudy canopy,
　　The wind his death-lament.
The ancient pulse of germ and birth
　　Was shrunken hard and dry,
And every spirit upon earth
　　Seemed fervourless as I.

At once a voice arose among
　　The bleak twigs overhead
In a full-hearted evensong
　　Of joy illimited;
An aged thrush, frail, gaunt, and small,
　　In blast-beruffled plume,

Had chosen thus to fling his soul
　　Upon the growing gloom.

So little cause for carolings
　　Of such ecstatic sound
Was written on terrestrial things
　　Afar or nigh around,
That I could think there trembled through
　　His happy good-night air
Some blessed Hope, whereof he knew
　　And I was unaware.

31 December 1900

GERARD MANLEY HOPKINS
(1844–1889)

THE WINDHOVER
to Christ Our Lord

I caught this morning morning's minion, king-
    dom of daylight's dauphin, dapple-dawn-drawn Falcon, in
      his riding
  Of the rolling level underneath him steady air, and striding
High there, how he rung upon the rein of a wimpling wing
In his ecstasy! then off, off forth on swing,
    As a skate's heel sweeps smooth on a bow-bend: the hurl and
      gliding
  Rebuffed the big wind. My heart in hiding
Stirred for a bird,—the achieve of, the mastery of the thing!

Brute beauty and valour and act, oh, air, pride, plume, here
    Buckle! AND the fire that breaks from thee then, a billion
Times told lovelier, more dangerous, O my chevalier!

    No wonder of it: shéer plód makes plough down sillion
Shine, and blue-bleak embers, ah my dear,
    Fall, gall themselves, and gash gold-vermilion.

THE WILD SWANS AT COOLE

The trees are in their autumn beauty,
The woodland paths are dry,
Under the October twilight the water
Mirrors a still sky;
Upon the brimming water among the stones
Are nine-and-fifty swans.

The nineteenth autumn has come upon me
Since I first made my count;
I saw, before I had well finished,
All suddenly mount
And scatter wheeling in great broken rings
Upon their clamorous wings.

I have looked upon those brilliant creatures,
And now my heart is sore.
All's changed since I, hearing at twilight,
The first time on this shore,
The bell-beat of their wings above my head,
Trod with a lighter tread.

Unwearied still, lover by lover,
They paddle in the cold
Companionable streams or climb the air;

Their hearts have not grown old;
Passion or conquest, wander where they will,
Attend upon them still.

But now they drift on the still water
Mysterious, beautiful;
Among what rushes will they build,
By what lake's edge or pool
Delight men's eyes when I awake some day
To find they have flown away?

FRANCIS JAMMES
(1868–1938)

A PRAYER TO GO TO PARADISE
WITH THE DONKEYS

to Máire and Jack

When I must come to you, O my God, I pray
It be some dusty-roaded holiday,
And even as in my travels here below,
I beg to choose by what road I shall go
To Paradise, where the clear stars shine by day.
I'll take my walking-stick and go my way,
And to my friends the donkeys I shall say,
"I am Francis Jammes, and I'm going to Paradise,
For there is no hell in the land of the loving God."
And I'll say to them: "Come, sweet friends of the blue skies,
Poor creatures who with a flap of the ears or a nod
Of the head shake off the buffets, the bees, the flies . . ."

Let me come with these donkeys, Lord, into your land,
These beasts who bow their heads so gently, and stand
With their small feet joined together in a fashion
Utterly gentle, asking your compassion.
I shall arrive, followed by their thousands of ears,
Followed by those with baskets at their flanks,
By those who lug the carts of mountebanks

Or loads of feather-dusters and kitchen-wares,
By those with humps of battered water-cans,
By bottle-shaped she-asses who halt and stumble,
By those tricked out in little pantaloons
To cover their wet, blue galls where flies assemble
In whirling swarms, making a drunken hum.
Dear God, let it be with these donkeys that I come,
And let it be that angels lead us in peace
To leafy streams where cherries tremble in air,
Sleek as the laughing flesh of girls; and there
In that haven of souls let it be that, leaning above
Your divine waters, I shall resemble these donkeys,
Whose humble and sweet poverty will appear
Clear in the clearness of your eternal love.

Translated by Richard Wilbur

ROBERT FROST
(1874–1963)

THE COW IN APPLE TIME

Something inspires the only cow of late
To make no more of a wall than an open gate,
And think no more of wall-builders than fools.
Her face is flecked with pomace and she drools
A cider syrup. Having tasted fruit,
She scorns a pasture withering to the root.
She runs from tree to tree where lie and sweeten
The windfalls spiked with stubble and worm-eaten.
She leaves them bitten when she has to fly.
She bellows on a knoll against the sky.
Her udder shrivels and the milk goes dry.

TWO LOOK AT TWO

Love and forgetting might have carried them
A little further up the mountainside
With night so near, but not much further up.
They must have halted soon in any case
With thoughts of the path back, how rough it was
With rock and washout, and unsafe in darkness;
When they were halted by a tumbled wall
With barbed-wire binding. They stood facing this,
Spending what onward impulse they still had
In one last look the way they must not go,
On up the failing path, where, if a stone
Or earthslide moved at night, it moved itself;
No footstep moved it. 'This is all,' they sighed,
'Good-night to woods.' But not so; there was more.
A doe from round a spruce stood looking at them
Across the wall, as near the wall as they.
She saw them in their field, they her in hers.
The difficulty of seeing what stood still,
Like some up-ended boulder split in two,
Was in her clouded eyes: they saw no fear there.
She seemed to think that two thus they were safe.
Then, as if they were something that, though strange,
She could not trouble her mind with too long,

She sighed and passed unscared along the wall.
'*This,* then, is all. What more is there to ask?'
But no, not yet. A snort to bid them wait.
A buck from round the spruce stood looking at them
Across the wall as near the wall as they.
This was an antlered buck of lusty nostril,
Not the same doe come back into her place.
He viewed them quizzically with jerks of head,
As if to ask 'Why don't you make some motion?
Or give some sign of life? Because you can't.
I doubt if you're as living as you look.'
Thus till he had them almost feeling dared
To stretch a proffering hand—and a spell-breaking.
Then he too passed unscared along the wall.
Two had seen two, whichever side you spoke from.
'This *must* be all.' It was all. Still they stood,
A great wave from it going over them,
As if the earth in one unlooked-for favor
Had made them certain earth returned their love.

THE SPAN OF LIFE

The old dog barks backward without getting up.
I can remember when he was a pup.

THE PANTHER

In the Jardin des Plantes, Paris

His vision, from the constantly passing bars,
has grown so weary that it cannot hold
anything else. It seems to him there are
a thousand bars; and behind the bars, no world.

As he paces in cramped circles, over and over,
the movement of his powerful soft strides
is like a ritual dance around a center
in which a mighty will stands paralyzed.

Only at times, the curtain of the pupils
lifts, quietly—. An image enters in,
rushes down through the tensed, arrested muscles,
plunges into the heart and is gone.

THE GAZELLE

Gazella Dorcas

Enchanted thing: how can two chosen words
ever attain the harmony of pure rhyme
that pulses through you as your body stirs?
Out of your forehead branch and lyre climb,

and all your features pass in simile, through
the songs of love whose words, as light as rose-
petals, rest on the face of someone who
has put his book away and shut his eyes:

to see you: tensed, as if each leg were a gun
loaded with leaps, but not fired while your neck
holds your head still, listening: as when,

while swimming in some isolated place,
a girl hears leaves rustle, and turns to look:
the forest pool reflected in her face.

THE LION CAGE

She paces back and forth like the sentinels out at the edge of the for-
tifications, where there is nothing left. And as in the sentinels, there
is homesickness in her, heavy homesickness in fragments.

As somewhere down in the ocean there must be mirrors, mirrors
from the cabins of sunken ships, fragments of mirrors, which of course
no longer contain anything: not the faces of the travelers, not one of
their gestures; not the way they turned and looked so strangely awk-
ward from the back; not the wall, not the corner where they slept;
still less what swayingly shone in from there and outside; nothing,
no. But as nevertheless a piece of seaweed perhaps, an open, sinking
polyp, the sudden face of a fish, or even just the water itself, floating,
parted, coming together again, evokes resemblances in those mirrors,
distant, oblique, false, soon abandoned resemblances with what once
existed—:

thus memories, fragments of memories, lie, broken-edged, in the
dark at the bottom of her blood.

She paces back and forth around him, the lion, who is sick. Being
sick doesn't concern him and doesn't diminish him; it just hems him
in. The way he lies, his soft bent paws intentionless, his proud face
heaped with a worn-out mane, his eyes no longer loaded, he is erected
upon himself as a monument to his own sadness, just as he once
(always beyond himself) was the exaggeration of his strength.

Now it still twitches here and there in his muscles, it tenses, here and there small spots of anger are forming, too distant from one another; the blood bursts angrily, with a leap, from the chambers of his heart, and certainly it still has its carefully tested turns of sudden decision when it rushes into the brain.

But he just lets things happen, because the end hasn't yet come, and he no longer exerts any energy and no longer takes part. Only far off, as though held away from himself, he paints with the soft paintbrush of his tail, again and again, a small, semicircular gesture of indescribable disdain. And this takes place so significantly that the lioness stops and looks over: troubled, aroused, expectant.

But then she begins her pacing again, the desperate, ridiculous pacing of the sentinel, which falls back into the same tracks, again and again. She paces and paces, and sometimes her distracted mask appears, round and full, crossed out by the bars.

She moves the way clocks move. And on her face, as on a clock dial which someone shines a light onto at night, a strange, briefly shown hour stands: a terrifying hour, in which someone dies.

THE FISHMONGER'S STALL

(Naples)

On a slightly inclined marble tabletop, they lie in groups, some on the damp stone, with a bit of blackish moss stuck under them, others in flat splint-baskets that have grown dark from the moisture. Silver-scaled, among them one that is bent upward like a sword arm in an escutcheon, so that the silver is stretched and shimmers. Silver-scaled, they lie across one another, as if of antique silver, with a blackish patina, and on top, one which, mouth forward, seems to be returning, terrified, out of the pile in back of it. Once you have noticed its mouth, you see, here and here, one more, another one, quickly turned toward you, lamenting. (What you want to call "lamenting" probably comes about because here the place from which voice emanates, at once means muteness: an image of the poet.) And now, as a result of a thought perhaps, you look for the eyes. All these flat, laterally placed eyes, covered as if with watch crystals, toward which, as long as they looked, floating images drifted. They weren't any different then, they were just as gazelessly indifferent: for water doesn't permit active looking. Just as shallow and depthless, empty, turned inside out like carriage lanterns during the day. But carried along by the resistance and movement of that denser world, they lightly and surely cast sketch upon sketch, signal and turn, inward into a consciousness unknown to us. Silently and surely they swam along, before the smooth decision, without betraying it; silently and surely they stood, for days on end, against the current, underneath its rush, darkened by fleeting shadows. But now they have been peeled out from the long strands of their looking, laid out flat, and it is impossible for anything to enter them. The pupil as if covered with black cloth, the surrounding circle laid on like the thinnest of gold foil. With a shock, as if you had bitten onto something hard, you notice the impenetrability of these eyes—, and suddenly you have the impression that you are standing in front of nothing but stone and metal, as you look across the table. Everything bent looks hard, and the pile of steel-glistening, awl-shaped fish lies there cold and heavy like a pile of tools with which others, that look like stones, have been polished. For there beside them they lie: round smooth agates, streaked with brown, pale, and golden veins, strips of reddish-white marble, jade pieces rounded and carefully polished, partly worked topazes, rock crystals with tips of amethyst, opals of jellyfish. And a very thin sheet of water is still spread over them all and separates them from this light, in which they are alien, closed, containers, which someone has tried in vain to pry open.

THE SWAN

This laboring through what is still undone,
as though, legs bound, we hobbled along the way,
is like the awkward walking of the swan.

And dying—to let go, no longer feel
the solid ground we stand on every day—
is like his anxious letting himself fall

into the water, which receives him gently
and which, as though with reverence and joy,
draws back past him in streams on either side;
while, infinitely silent and aware,
in his full majesty and ever more
indifferent, he condescends to glide.

BLACK CAT

A ghost, though invisible, still is like a place
your sight can knock on, echoing; but here
within this thick black pelt, your strongest gaze
will be absorbed and utterly disappear:

just as a raving madman, when nothing else
can ease him, charges into his dark night
howling, pounds on the padded wall, and feels
the rage being taken in and pacified.

She seems to hide all looks that have ever fallen
into her, so that, like an audience,
she can look them over, menacing and sullen,
and curl to sleep with them. But all at once

as if awakened, she turns her face to yours;
and with a shock, you see yourself, tiny,
inside the golden amber of her eyeballs
suspended, like a prehistoric fly.

THE FLAMINGOS

Jardin des Plantes, Paris

With all the subtle paints of Fragonard
no more of their red and white could be expressed
than someone would convey about his mistress
by telling you, "She was lovely, lying there

still soft with sleep." They rise above the green
grass and lightly sway on their long pink stems,
side by side, like enormous feathery blossoms,
seducing (more seductively than Phryne)

themselves; till, necks curling, they sink their large
pale eyes into the softness of their down,
where apple-red and jet-black lie concealed.

A shriek of envy shakes the parrot cage;
but *they* stretch out, astonished, and one by one
stride into their imaginary world.

THE EIGHTH DUINO ELEGY

Dedicated to Rudolf Kassner

With all its eyes the natural world looks out
into the Open. Only *our* eyes are turned
backward, and surround plant, animal, child
like traps, as they emerge into their freedom.
We know what is really out there only from
the animal's gaze; for we take the very young
child and force it around, so that it sees
objects—not the Open, which is so
deep in animals' faces. Free from death.
We, only, can see death; the free animal
has its decline in back of it, forever,
and God in front, and when it moves, it moves
already in eternity, like a fountain.

Never, not for a single day, do *we* have
before us that pure space into which flowers
endlessly open. Always there is World
and never Nowhere without the No: that pure
unseparated element which one breathes
without desire and endlessly *knows*. A child
may wander there for hours, through the timeless

stillness, may get lost in it and be
shaken back. Or someone dies and *is* it.
For, nearing death, one doesn't see death; but stares
beyond, perhaps with an animal's vast gaze.
Lovers, if the beloved were not there
blocking the view, are close to it, and marvel ...
As if by some mistake, it opens for them
behind each other ... But neither can move past
the other, and it changes back to World.
Forever turned toward objects, we see in them
the mere reflection of the realm of freedom,
which we have dimmed. Or when some animal
mutely, serenely, looks us through and through.
That is what fate means: to be opposite,
to be opposite and nothing else, forever.

If the animal moving toward us so securely
in a different direction had our kind of
consciousness—, it would wrench us around and drag us
along its path. But it feels its life as boundless,
unfathomable, and without regard
to its own condition: pure, like its outward gaze.
And where we see the future, it sees all time
and itself within all time, forever healed.

Yet in the alert, warm animal there lies
the pain and burden of an enormous sadness.
For it too feels the presence of what often
overwhelms us: a memory, as if
the element we keep pressing toward was once
more intimate, more true, and our communion
infinitely tender. Here all is distance;
there it was breath. After that first home,
the second seems ambiguous and drafty.

Oh bliss of the *tiny* creature which remains
forever inside the womb that was its shelter;
joy of the gnat which, still *within,* leaps up
even at its marriage: for everything is womb.
And look at the half-assurance of the bird,
which knows both inner and outer, from its source,
as if it were the soul of an Etruscan,
flown out of a dead man received inside a space,
but with his reclining image as the lid.
And how bewildered is any womb-born creature
that has to fly. As if terrified and fleeing
from itself, it zigzags through the air, the way
a crack runs through a teacup. So the bat
quivers across the porcelain of evening.

And we: spectators, always, everywhere,
turned toward the world of objects, never outward.
It fills us. We arrange it. It breaks down.
We rearrange it, then break down ourselves.

Who has twisted us around like this, so that
no matter what we do, we are in the posture
of someone going away? Just as, upon
the farthest hill, which shows him his whole valley
one last time, he turns, stops, lingers—,
so we live here, forever taking leave.

THE SONNETS TO ORPHEUS I, 20

But Master, what gift shall I dedicate to you,
who taught all creatures their ears?
—My thoughts of an evening long ago,
it was springtime, in Russia—a horse . . .

He came bounding from the village, alone, white,
with a hobble attached to one leg,
to stay alone in the fields all night;
how the mane beat against his neck

to the rhythm of his perfect joy, in that hindered
gallop across the meadow.
What leaping went on in his stallion-blood!

He felt the expanses, and oh!
He sang and he heard—your cycle of myths
was completed in him.

His image: my gift.

"FARFALLETTINA"

Shaking all over, she arrives near the lamp, and her dizziness grants her one last vague reprieve before she goes up in flames. She has fallen onto the green tablecloth, and upon that advantageous background she stretches out for a moment (for a unit of her own time which we have no way of measuring) the profusion of her inconceivable splendor. She looks like a miniature lady who is having a heart attack on the way to the theater. She will never arrive. Besides, where is there a theater for such fragile spectators? . . . Her wings, with their tiny golden threads, are moving like a double fan in front of no face; and between them is this thin body, a bilboquet onto which two eyes like emerald balls have fallen back . . .

It is in you, my dear, that God has exhausted himself. He tosses you into the fire so that he can recover a bit of his strength. (Like a little boy breaking into his piggy bank.)

THE BULL

It is in captivity—
ringed, haltered, chained
to a drag
the bull is godlike

Unlike the cows
he lives alone, nozzles
the sweet grass gingerly
to pass the time away

He kneels, lies down
and stretching out
a foreleg licks himself
about the hoof

then stays
with half-closed eyes,
Olympian commentary on
the bright passage of days.

—The round sun
smooths his lacquer
through
the glossy pinetrees

his substance hard
as ivory or glass—
through which the wind
yet plays—
                Milkless

he nods
the hair between his horns
and eyes matted
with hyacinthine curls

POEM

As the cat
climbed over
the top of

the jamcloset
first the right
forefoot

carefully
then the hind
stepped down

into the pit of
the empty
flowerpot

THE SPARROW

(To My Father)

This sparrow
      who comes to sit at my window
            is a poetic truth
more than a natural one.
      His voice,
            his movements,
his habits—
      how he loves to
            flutter his wings
in the dust—
      all attest it;
            granted, he does it
to rid himself of lice
      but the relief he feels
            makes him
cry out lustily—
      which is a trait
            more related to music
than otherwise.
      Wherever he finds himself
            in early spring,

on back streets
        or beside palaces,
                he carries on
unaffectedly
        his amours.
                It begins in the egg,
his sex genders it:
        What is more pretentiously
                useless
or about which
        we more pride ourselves?
                It leads as often as not
to our undoing.
        The cockerel, the crow
                with their challenging voices
cannot surpass
        the insistence
                of his cheep!
Once
        at El Paso
                toward evening,
I saw—and heard!—
        ten thousand sparrows
                who had come in from
the desert
        to roost. They filled the trees
                of a small park. Men fled
(with ears ringing!)
        from their droppings,
                leaving the premises
to the alligators
        who inhabit
                the fountain. His image

is familiar
              as that of the aristocratic
                            unicorn, a pity
there are not more oats eaten
              nowadays
                            to make living easier
for him.
              At that,
                            his small size,
keen eyes,
              serviceable beak
                            and general truculence
assure his survival—
              to say nothing
                            of his innumerable
brood.
              Even the Japanese
                            know him
and have painted him
              sympathetically,
                            with profound insight
into his minor
              characteristics.
                            Nothing even remotely
subtle
              about his lovemaking.
                            He crouches
before the female,
              drags his wings,
                            waltzing,
throws back his head
              and simply—
                            yells! The din

is terrific.
   The way he swipes his bill
    across a plank
to clean it,
   is decisive.
     So with everything
he does. His coppery
   eyebrows
     give him the air
of being always
   a winner—and yet
    I saw once,
the female of his species
   clinging determinedly
    to the edge of
a water pipe,
   catch him
    by his crown-feathers
to hold him
   silent,
    subdued,
hanging above the city streets
   until
    she was through with him.
What was the use
   of that?
    She hung there
herself,
   puzzled at her success.
    I laughed heartily.
Practical to the end,
   it is the poem
    of his existence

that triumphed
      finally;
            a wisp of feathers
flattened to the pavement,
      wings spread symmetrically
         as if in flight,
the head gone,
      the black escutcheon of the breast
         undecipherable,
an effigy of a sparrow,
      a dried wafer only,
         left to say
and it says it
      without offense,
         beautifully;
This was I,
      a sparrow.
         I did my best;
farewell.

STORMY

what name could
better
explode from

a sleeping pup
but this
leaping

to his feet
Stormy!
Stormy! Stormy!

THE TURTLE

(For My Grandson)

Not because of his eyes,
    the eyes of a bird,
        but because he is beaked,
birdlike, to do an injury,
    has the turtle attracted you.
        He is your only pet.
When we are together
    you talk of nothing else
        ascribing all sorts
of murderous motives
    to his least action.
        You ask me
to write a poem,
    should I have poems to write,
        about a turtle.

The turtle lives in the mud
    but is not mud-like,
        you can tell it by his eyes
which are clear.
    When he shall escape
        his present confinement

he will stride about the world
        destroying all
                with his sharp beak.
Whatever opposes him
        in the streets of the city
                shall go down.
Cars will be overturned.
        And upon his back
                shall ride,
to his conquests,
        my Lord,
                you!

You shall be master!
        In the beginning
                there was a great tortoise
who supported the world.
        Upon him
                all ultimately
rests.
        Without him
                nothing will stand.
He is all wise
        and can outrun the hare.
                In the night
his eyes carry him
        to unknown places.
                He is your friend.

D. H. LAWRENCE
(1885–1930)

THE MOSQUITO

When did you start your tricks,
Monsieur?

What do you stand on such high legs for?
Why this length of shredded shank,
You exaltation?

Is it so that you shall lift your centre of gravity upwards
And weigh no more than air as you alight upon me,
Stand upon me weightless, you phantom?

I heard a woman call you the Winged Victory
In sluggish Venice.
You turn your head towards your tail, and smile.

How can you put so much devilry
Into that translucent phantom shred
Of a frail corpus?

Queer, with your thin wings and your streaming legs,
How you sail like a heron, or a dull clot of air,
A nothingness.

Yet what an aura surrounds you;
Your evil little aura, prowling, and casting a numbness on my mind.

That is your trick, your bit of filthy magic:
Invisibility, and the anæsthetic power
To deaden my attention in your direction.

But I know your game now, streaky sorcerer.
Queer, how you stalk and prowl the air
In circles and evasions, enveloping me,
Ghoul on wings
Winged Victory.

Settle, and stand on long thin shanks
Eyeing me sideways, and cunningly conscious that I am aware,
You speck.

I hate the way you lurch off sideways into air
Having read my thoughts against you.

Come then, let us play at unawares,
And see who wins this sly game of bluff.
Man or mosquito.

You don't know that I exist, and I don't know that you exist.
Now then!

It is your trump.
It is your hateful little trump,
You pointed fiend,
Which shakes my sudden blood to hatred of you:
It is your small, high, hateful bugle in my ear.

Why do you do it?
Surely it is bad policy.

They say you can't help it.

If that is so, then I believe a little in Providence protecting the innocent.
But it sounds so amazingly like a slogan,
A yell of triumph as you snatch my scalp.

Blood, red blood
Super-magical
Forbidden liquor.

I behold you stand
For a second enspasmed in oblivion,
Obscenely ecstasied
Sucking live blood,
My blood.

Such silence, such suspended transport,
Such gorging,
Such obscenity of trespass.

You stagger
As well as you may.
Only your accused hairy frailty,
Your own imponderable weightlessness
Saves you, wafts you away on the very draught my anger makes in
    its snatching.

Away with a pæan of derision,
You winged blood-drop.

Can I not overtake you?
Are you one too many for me,
Winged Victory?
Am I not mosquito enough to out-mosquito you?

Queer, what a big stain my sucked blood makes
Beside the infinitesimal faint smear of you!
Queer, what a dim dark smudge you have disappeared into!

SNAKE

A snake came to my water-trough
On a hot, hot day, and I in pyjamas for the heat,
To drink there.

In the deep, strange-scented shade of the great dark carob-tree
I came down the steps with my pitcher
And must wait, must stand and wait, for there he was at the trough
    before me.

He reached down from a fissure in the earth-wall in the gloom
And trailed his yellow-brown slackness soft-bellied down, over the
    edge of the stone trough
And rested his throat upon the stone bottom,
And where the water had dripped from the tap, in a small clearness,
He sipped with his straight mouth,
Softly drank through his straight gums, into his slack long body,
Silently.

Someone was before me at my water-trough,
And I, like a second comer, waiting.

He lifted his head from his drinking, as cattle do,
And looked at me vaguely, as drinking cattle do,
And flickered his two-forked tongue from his lips, and mused a
    moment,

And stooped and drank a little more,
Being earth-brown, earth-golden from the burning bowels of the
    earth
On the day of Sicilian July, with Etna smoking.

The voice of my education said to me
He must be killed,
For in Sicily the black, black snakes are innocent, the gold are
    venomous.

And voices in me said, If you were a man
You would take a stick and break him now, and finish him off.

But must I confess how I liked him,
How glad I was he had come like a guest in quiet, to drink at my
    water-trough
And depart peaceful, pacified, and thankless,
Into the burning bowels of this earth?

Was it cowardice, that I dared not kill him?
Was it perversity, that I longed to talk to him?
Was it humility, to feel so honoured?
I felt so honoured.

And yet those voices:
If you were not afraid, you would kill him!

And truly I was afraid, I was most afraid,
But even so, honoured still more
That he should seek out my hospitality
From out the dark door of the secret earth.

He drank enough
And lifted his head, dreamily, as one who has drunken,
And flickered his tongue like a forked night on the air, so black,
Seeming to lick his lips,

And looked around like a god, unseeing, into the air,
And slowly turned his head,
And slowly, very slowly, as if thrice adream,
Proceeded to draw his slow length curving round
And climb again the broken bank of my wall-face.

And as he put his head into that dreadful hole,
And as he slowly drew up, snake-easing his shoulders, and entered
    farther,
A sort of horror, a sort of protest against his withdrawing into that
    horrid black hole,
Deliberately going into the blackness, and slowly drawing himself
    after,
Overcame me now his back was turned.

I looked round, I put down my pitcher,
I picked up a clumsy log
And threw it at the water-trough with a clatter.

I think it did not hit him,
But suddenly that part of him that was left behind convulsed in
    undignified haste,
Writhed like lightning, and was gone
Into the black hole, the earth-lipped fissure in the wall-front,
At which, in the intense still noon, I stared with fascination.

And immediately I regretted it.
I thought how paltry, how vulgar, what a mean act!
I despised myself and the voices of my accursed human education.

And I thought of the albatross,
And I wished he would come back, my snake.

For he seemed to me again like a king,
Like a king in exile, uncrowned in the underworld,
Now due to be crowned again.

And so, I missed my chance with one of the lords
Of life.
And I have something to expiate;
A pettiness.

BABY TORTOISE

You know what it is to be born alone,
Baby tortoise!

The first day to heave your feet little by little from the shell,
Not yet awake,
And remain lapsed on earth,
Not quite alive.

A tiny, fragile, half-animate bean.

To open your tiny beak-mouth, that looks as if it would never open,
Like some iron door;
To lift the upper hawk-beak from the lower base
And reach your skinny little neck
And take your first bite at some dim bit of herbage,
Alone, small insect,
Tiny bright-eye,
Slow one.

To take your first solitary bite
And move on your slow, solitary hunt.
Your bright, dark little eye,
Your eye of a dark disturbed night,

Under its slow lid, tiny baby tortoise,
So indomitable.

No one ever heard you complain.

You draw your head forward, slowly, from your little wimple
And set forward, slow-dragging, on your four-pinned toes,
Rowing slowly forward.
Whither away, small bird?

Rather like a baby working its limbs,
Except that you make slow, ageless progress
And a baby makes none.

The touch of sun excites you,
And the long ages, and the lingering chill
Make you pause to yawn,
Opening your impervious mouth,
Suddenly beak-shaped, and very wide, like some suddenly gaping
    pincers;
Soft red tongue, and hard thin gums,
Then close the wedge of your little mountain front,
Your face, baby tortoise.

Do you wonder at the world, as slowly you turn your head in its
    wimple
And look with laconic, black eyes?
Or is it sleep coming over you again,
The non-life?

You are so hard to wake.

Are you able to wonder?
Or is it just your indomitable will and pride of the first life
Looking round

And slowly pitching itself against the inertia
Which had seemed invincible?

The vast inanimate,
And the fine brilliance of your so tiny eye,
Challenger.

Nay, tiny shell-bird,
What a huge vast inanimate it is, that you must row against,
What an incalculable inertia.

Challenger,
Little Ulysses, fore-runner,
No bigger than my thumb-nail,
Buon viaggio.

All animate creation on your shoulder,
Set forth, little Titan, under your battle-shield.

The ponderous, preponderate,
Inanimate universe;
And you are slowly moving, pioneer, you alone.

How vivid your travelling seems now, in the troubled sunshine,
Stoic, Ulyssean atom;
Suddenly hasty, reckless, on high toes.

Voiceless little bird,
Resting your head half out of your wimple
In the slow dignity of your eternal pause.
Alone, with no sense of being alone,
And hence six times more solitary;
Fulfilled of the slow passion of pitching through immemorial ages
Your little round house in the midst of chaos.

Over the garden earth,
Small bird,
Over the edge of all things.

Traveller,
With your tail tucked a little on one side
Like a gentleman in a long-skirted coat.

All life carried on your shoulder,
Invincible fore-runner.

HUMMING-BIRD

I can imagine, in some otherworld
Primeval-dumb, far back
In that most awful stillness, that only gasped and hummed,
Humming-birds raced down the avenues.

Before anything had a soul,
When life was a heave of Matter, half inanimate,
This little bit chipped off in brilliance
And went whizzing through the slow, vast, succulent stems.

I believe there were no flowers then,
In the world where the humming-bird flashed ahead of creation.
I believe he pierced the slow vegetable veins with his long beak.

Probably he was big
As mosses, and little lizards, they say, were once big.
Probably he was a jabbing, terrifying monster.

We look at him through the wrong end of the long telescope of Time,
Luckily for us.

SHE-GOAT

Goats go past the back of the house like dry leaves in the dawn,
And up the hill like a river, if you watch.

At dusk they patter back like a bough being dragged on the ground,
Raising dusk and acridity of goats, and bleating.

Our old goat we tie up at night in the shed at the back of the
    broken Greek tomb in the garden,
And when the herd goes by at dawn she begins to bleat for me to
    come down and untie her.

Merr — err — err! Merr — er — errr! Mer! Mé!
—Wait, wait a bit, I'll come when I've lit the fire.
Merrr!
—Exactly.
Mé! Mer! Merrrrrrr!!!
—Tace, tu, crapa, bestia!
Merr — ererr — ererrrr! Merrrr!

She is such an alert listener, with her ears wide, to know am I coming!
Such a canny listener, from a distance, looking upwards, lending
    first one ear, then another.

There she is, perched on her manger, looking over the boards into
    the day
Like a belle at her window.
And immediately she sees me she blinks, stares, doesn't know me,
    turns her head and ignores me vulgarly with a wooden blank on
    her face.

What do I care for her, the ugly female, standing up there with her
    long tangled sides like an old rug thrown over a fence.
But she puts her nose down shrewdly enough when the knot is untied,
And jumps staccato to earth, a sharp, dry jump, still ignoring me,
Pretending to look round the stall.

Come on, you, crapa! I'm not your servant!

She turns her head away with an obtuse, female sort of deafness, bête.
And then invariably she crouches her rear and makes water.
That being her way of answer, if I speak to her. —Self-conscious!
Le bestie non parlano, poverine!

She was bought at Giardini fair, on the sands, for six hundred lire.

An obstinate old witch, almost jerking the rope from my hands to
    eat the acanthus, or bite at the almond buds, and make me wait.
Yet the moment I hate her she trips mild and smug like a woman
    going to mass.
The moment I really detest her.

Queer it is, suddenly, in the garden
To catch sight of her standing like some huge, ghoulish grey bird in
    the air, on the bough of the leaning almond-tree,
Straight as a board on the bough, looking down like some hairy
    horrid God the Father in a William Blake imagination.
Come down, crapa, out of that almond-tree!

Instead of which she strangely rears on her perch in the air, vast
    beast,
And strangely paws the air, delicate,
And reaches her black-striped face up like a snake, far up,
Subtly, to the twigs overhead, far up, vast beast,
And snaps them sharp, with a little twist of her anaconda head;
All her great hairy-shaggy belly open against the morning.

At seasons she curls back her tail like a green leaf in the fire,
Or like a lifted hand, hailing at her wrong end.
And having exposed the pink place of her nakedness, fixedly,
She trots on blithe toes,
And if you look at her, she looks back with a cold, sardonic stare.
Sardonic, sardonyx, rock of cold fire.
See me? She says, *That's me!*

That's her.

Then she leaps the rocks like a quick rock,
Her backbone sharp as a rock,
Sheer will.

Along which ridge of libidinous magnetism
Defiant, curling the leaf of her tail as if she were curling her lip
    behind her at all life,
Libidinous desire runs back and forth, asserting itself in that
    little lifted bare hand.

Yet she has such adorable spurty kids, like spurts of black ink.
And in a month again is as if she had never had them.

And when the billy goat mounts her
She is brittle as brimstone.
While his slitted eyes squint back to the roots of his ears.

KANGAROO

In the northern hemisphere
Life seems to leap at the air, or skim under the wind
Like stags on rocky ground, or pawing horses, or springy scut-tailed
    rabbits.

Or else rush horizontal to charge at the sky's horizon,
Like bulls or bisons or wild pigs.

Or slip like water slippery towards its ends,
As foxes, stoats, and wolves, and prairie dogs.

Only mice, and moles, and rats, and badgers, and beavers, and
    perhaps bears
Seem belly-plumbed to the earth's mid-navel.
Or frogs that when they leap come flop, and flop to the centre of
    the earth.

But the yellow antipodal Kangaroo, when she sits up,
Who can unseat her, like a liquid drop that is heavy, and just touches
    earth.

The downward drip
The down-urge.
So much denser than cold-blooded frogs.

Delicate mother Kangaroo
Sitting up there rabbit-wise, but huge, plumb-weighted,
And lifting her beautiful slender face, oh! so much more gently and
 finely lined than a rabbit's, or than a hare's,
Lifting her face to nibble at a round white peppermint drop which
 she loves, sensitive mother Kangaroo.

Her sensitive, long, pure-bred face,
Her full antipodal eyes, so dark,
So big and quiet and remote, having watched so many empty dawns
 in silent Australia.

Her little loose hands, and drooping Victorian shoulders.
And then her great weight below the waist, her vast pale belly,
With a thin young yellow little paw hanging out, and straggle of a
 long thin ear, like ribbon,
Like a funny trimming to the middle of her belly, thin little dangle
 of an immature paw, and one thin ear.

Her belly, her big haunches
And, in addition, the great muscular python-stretch of her tail.

There, she shan't have any more peppermint drops.
So she wistfully, sensitively sniffs the air, and then turns, goes off in
 slow sad leaps

On the long flat skis of her legs,
Steered and propelled by that steel-strong snake of a tail.

Stops again, half turns, inquisitive to look back.
While something stirs quickly in her belly, and a lean little face
 comes out, as from a window,
Peaked and a bit dismayed,
Only to disappear again quickly away from the sight of the world,
 to snuggle down in the warmth,
Leaving the trail of a different paw hanging out.

Still she watches with eternal, cocked wistfulness!
How full her eyes are, like the full, fathomless, shining eyes of an
    Australian black-boy
Who has been lost so many centuries on the margins of existence!

She watches with insatiable wistfulness.
Untold centuries of watching for something to come,
For a new signal from life, in that silent lost land of the South.

Where nothing bites but insects and snakes and the sun, small life.
Where no bull roared, no cow ever lowed, no stag cried, no leopard
    screeched, no lion coughed, no dog barked,
But all was silent save for parrots occasionally, in the haunted blue
    bush.

Wistfully watching, with wonderful liquid eyes.
And all her weight, all her blood, dripping sack-wise down towards
    the earth's centre,
And the live little-one taking in its paw at the door of her belly.

Leap then, and come down on the line that draws to the earth's deep,
    heavy centre.

ROBINSON JEFFERS
(1887–1962)

BIRDS

The fierce musical cries of a couple of sparrowhawks hunting on the
    headland,
Hovering and darting, their heads northwestward,
Prick like silver arrows shot through a curtain the noise of the ocean
Trampling its granite; their red backs gleam
Under my window around the stone corners; nothing gracefuller, nothing
    nothing
Nimbler in the wind. Westward the wave-gleaners,
The old gray sea-going gulls are gathered together, the northwest
    wind wakening
Their wings to the wild spirals of the wind-dance.
Fresh as the air, salt as the foam, play birds in the bright wind, fly
    falcons
Forgetting the oak and the pinewood, come gulls
From the Carmel sands and the sands at the river-mouth, from
    Lobos and out of the limitless
Power of the mass of the sea, for a poem
Needs multitude, multitudes of thoughts, all fierce, all flesh-eaters,
    musically clamorous
Bright hawks that hover and dart headlong, and ungainly
Gray hungers fledged with desire of transgression, salt slimed beaks,
    from the sharp
Rock-shores of the world and the secret waters.

PELICANS

Four pelicans went over the house,
Sculled their worn oars over the courtyard: I saw that ungainliness
Magnifies the idea of strength.
A lifting gale of sea-gulls followed them; slim yachts of the element,
Natural growths of the sky, no wonder
Light wings to leave sea; but those grave weights toil, and are
    powerful,
And the wings torn with old storms remember
The cone that the oldest redwood dropped from, the tilting of
    continents,
The dinosaur's day, the lift of new sea-lines.
The omnisecular spirit keeps the old with the new also.
Nothing at all has suffered erasure.
There is life not of our time. He calls ungainly bodies
As beautiful as the grace of horses.
He is weary of nothing; he watches air-planes; he watches pelicans.

HURT HAWKS

I

The broken pillar of the wing jags from the clotted shoulder,
The wing trails like a banner in defeat,
No more to use the sky forever but live with famine
And pain a few days: cat nor coyote
Will shorten the week of waiting for death, there is game without
    talons.
He stands under the oak-bush and waits
The lame feet of salvation; at night he remembers freedom
And flies in a dream, the dawns ruin it.
He is strong and pain is worse to the strong, incapacity is worse.
The curs of the day come and torment him
At distance, no one but death the redeemer will humble that head,
The intrepid readiness, the terrible eyes.
The wild God of the world is sometimes merciful to those
That ask mercy, not often to the arrogant.
You do not know him, you communal people, or you have
    forgotten him;
Intemperate and savage, the hawk remembers him;
Beautiful and wild, the hawks, and men that are dying, remember
    him.

II

I'd sooner, except the penalties, kill a man than a hawk; but the
    great redtail
Had nothing left but unable misery
From the bones too shattered for mending, the wing that trailed
    under his talons when he moved.
We had fed him six weeks, I gave him freedom,
He wandered over the foreland hill and returned in the evening,
    asking for death,
Not like a beggar, still eyed with the old
Implacable arrogance. I gave him the lead gift in the twilight. What
    fell was relaxed,
Owl-downy, soft feminine feathers; but what
Soared: the fierce rush: the night-herons by the flooded river cried
    fear at its rising
Before it was quite unsheathed from reality.

MARIANNE MOORE

(1887–1972)

THE FRIGATE PELICAN

Rapidly cruising or lying on the air there is a bird
    that realizes Rasselas's friend's project
    of wings uniting levity with strength. This
        hell-diver, frigate-bird, hurricane-
bird; unless swift is the proper word
        for him, the storm omen when
    he flies close to the waves, should be seen
        fishing, although oftener
        he appears to prefer

to take, on the wing, from industrious crude-winged species
    the fish they have caught, and is seldom successless.
    A marvel of grace, no matter how fast his
        victim may fly or how often may
turn. The others with similar ease,
    slowly rising once more,
        move out to the top
        of the circle and stop

and blow back, allowing the wind to reverse their direction—
    Unlike the more stalwart swan that can ferry the
    woodcutter's two children home. Make hay; keep
        the shop; I have one sheep; were a less

limber animal's mottoes. This one
        finds sticks for the swan's-down-dress
of his child to rest upon and would
        not know Gretel from Hänsel.
        As impassioned Handel—

meant for a lawyer and a masculine German domestic
    career—clandestinely studied the harpsichord
    and never was known to have fallen in love,
        the unconfiding frigate-bird hides
in the height and in the majestic
        display of his art. He glides
    a hundred feet or quivers about
            as charred paper behaves—full
            of feints; and an eagle

of vigilance.... *Festina lente.* Be gay
    civilly? How so? 'If I do well I am blessed
    whether any bless me or not, and if I do
        ill I am cursed.' We watch the moon rise
on the Susquehanna. In his way,
        this most romantic bird flies
    to a more mundane place, the mangrove
            swamp to sleep. He wastes the moon.
            But he, and others, soon

rise from the bough and though flying, are able to foil the tired
    moment of danger that lays on heart and lungs the
    weight of the python that crushes to powder.

THE MONKEYS

winked too much and were afraid of snakes. The zebras, supreme in
their abnormality; the elephants with their fog-coloured skin
    and strictly practical appendages
        were there, the small cats; and the parrakeet—
            trivial and humdrum on examination, destroying
        bark and portions of the food it could not eat.

I recall their magnificence, now not more magnificent
than it is dim. It is difficult to recall the ornament,
    speech, and precise manner of what one might
        call the minor acquaintances twenty
            years back; but I shall not forget him—that Gilgamesh among
        the hairy carnivora—that cat with the

wedge-shaped, slate-grey marks on its forelegs and the resolute tail,
astringently remarking, 'They have imposed on us with their pale
    half-fledged protestations, trembling about
        in inarticulate frenzy, saying
            it is not for us to understand art; finding it
        all so difficult, examining the thing

as if it were inconceivably arcanic, as symmet-
rically frigid as if it had been carved out of chrysoprase
    or marble—strict with tension, malignant

in its power over us and deeper
than the sea when it proffers flattery in exchange for hemp,
rye, flax, horses, platinum, timber, and fur.'

PETER

Strong and slippery, built for the midnight grass-party confronted by
　　　　　　　　　　　　　　　four cats,
　he sleeps his time away—the detached first claw on the foreleg,
　　　　　　　　　　　which corresponds
　　to the thumb, retracted to its tip; the small tuft of fronds
　　　or katydid-legs above each eye, still numbering the units in each
　　　　　　　　　　　　　　group;
　　　　the shadbones regularly set about the mouth, to droop or rise

in unison like the porcupine's quills—motionless. He lets himself be flat-
　tened out by gravity, as it were a piece of seaweed tamed and
　　　　　　　　　　　weakened by
　　exposure to the sun; compelled when extended, to lie
　　　stationary. Sleep is the result of his delusion that one must do as
　　　　well as one can for oneself; sleep—epitome of what is to

him as to the average person, the end of life. Demonstrate on him how
　the lady caught the dangerous southern snake, placing a forked stick
　　　　　　　　　　　on either
　　side of its innocuous neck; one need not try to stir
　　　him up; his prune-shaped head and alligator eyes are not a party
　　　　　　　　　　　to the
　　　　joke. Lifted and handled, he may be dangled like an eel or set

up on the forearm like a mouse; his eyes bisected by pupils of a pin's
    width, are flickeringly exhibited, then covered up. May be? I should say
    might have been; when he has been got the better of in a
        dream—as in a fight with nature or with cats—we all know it.
                                           Profound sleep is
        not with him a fixed illusion. Springing about with froglike ac-

curacy, emitting jerky cries when taken in the hand, he is himself
    again; to sit caged by the rungs of a domestic chair would be
                                      unprofit-
able—human. What is the good of hypocrisy? It
    is permissible to choose one's employment, to abandon the wire
                                      nail, the
    roly-poly, when it shows signs of being no longer a pleas-

ure, to score the adjacent magazine with a double line of strokes. He can
    talk, but insolently says nothing. What of it? When one is frank,
                                  one's very
    presence is a compliment. It is clear that he can see
        the virtue of naturalness, that he is one of those who do not regard
        the published fact as a surrender. As for the disposition

invariably to affront, an animal with claws wants to have to use
    them; that eel-like extension of trunk into tail is not an accident. To
    leap, to lengthen out, divide the air—to purloin, to pursue.
        To tell the hen: fly over the fence, go in the wrong way in your
                                    perturba-
        tion—this is life; to do less would be nothing but dishonesty.

HE 'DIGESTETH HARDE YRON'

Although the aepyornis
        or roc that lived in Madagascar, and
the moa are extinct,
the camel-sparrow, linked
        with them in size—the large sparrow
Xenophon saw walking by a stream—was and is
a symbol of justice.

This bird watches his chicks with
        a maternal concentration—and he's
been mothering the eggs
at night six weeks—his legs
        their only weapon of defence.
He is swifter than a horse; he has a foot hard
as a hoof; the leopard

is not more suspicious. How
        could he, prized for plumes and eggs and young, used
even as a riding-
beast, respect men hiding
        actor-like in ostrich-skins, with
the right hand making the neck move as if alive and
from a bag the left hand

strewing grain, that ostriches
　　might be decoyed and killed! Yes this is he
whose plume was anciently
the plume of justice; he
　　whose comic duckling head on its
great neck revolves with compass-needle nervousness
when he stands guard, in S-

　　like foragings as he is
　　preening the down on his leaden-skinned back.
The egg piously shown
as Leda's very own
　　from which Castor and Pollux hatched,
was an ostrich-egg. And what could have been more fit
for the Chinese lawn it

　　grazed on as a gift to an
　　emperor who admired strange birds, than this
one who builds his mud-made
nest in dust yet will wade
　　in lake or sea till only the head shows.

　　　　·　　　·　　　·　　　·　　　·　　　·

　　Six hundred ostrich-brains served
　　　　at one banquet, the ostrich-plume-tipped tent
and desert spear, jewel-
gorgeous ugly egg-shell
　　goblets, eight pairs of ostriches
in harness, dramatize a meaning always missed
by the externalist.

　　The power of the visible
　　is the invisible; as even where
no tree of freedom grows,

so-called brute courage knows.
    Heroism is exhausting, yet
it contradicts a greed that did not wisely spare
the harmless solitaire

    or great auk in its grandeur;
    unsolicitude having swallowed up
all giant birds but an
alert gargantuan
    little-winged, magnificently speedy running-bird. This one
remaining rebel
is the sparrow-camel.

BIRD-WITTED

With innocent wide penguin eyes, three
    large fledgling mocking-birds below
the pussy-willow tree,
    stand in a row,
wings touching, feebly solemn,
till they see
        their no longer larger
        mother bringing
something which will partially
feed one of them.

Toward the high-keyed intermittent squeak
    of broken carriage-springs, made by
the three similar, meek-
    coated bird's-eye
freckled forms she comes; and when
from the beak
        of one, the still living
        beetle has dropped
out, she picks it up and puts
it in again.

Standing in the shade till they have dressed
    their thickly-filamented, pale

pussy-willow-surfaced
    coats, they spread tail
and wings, showing one by one,
the modest
        white stripe lengthwise on the
        tail and crosswise
underneath the wing, and the
accordion

is closed again. What delightful note
    with rapid unexpected flute-
sounds leaping from the throat
    of the astute
grown bird, comes back to one from
the remote
        unenergetic sun-
        lit air before
the brood was here? How harsh
the bird's voice has become.

A piebald cat observing them,
    is slowly creeping toward the trim
trio on the tree-stem.
    Unused to him
the three make room—uneasy
new problem.
        A dangling foot that missed
        its grasp, is raised
and finds the twig on which it
planned to perch. The

parent darting down, nerved by what chills
    the blood, and by hope rewarded—
of toil—since nothing fills
    squeaking unfed

mouths, wages deadly combat,
and half kills
      with bayonet beak and
      cruel wings, the
intellectual cautious-
ly creeping cat.

THE PANGOLIN

Another armoured animal—scale
    lapping scale with spruce-cone regularity until they
form the uninterrupted central
    tail-row! This near artichoke with head and legs and grit-equipped
                   gizzard,
    the night miniature artist engineer is
        Leonardo's—da Vinci's replica—
           impressive animal and toiler of whom we seldom hear.
        Armour seems extra. But for him,
          the closing ear-ridge—
             or bare ear lacking even this small
             eminence and similarly safe

contracting nose and eye apertures
        impenetrably closable, are not;—a true ant-eater,
not cockroach-eater, who endures
    exhausting solitary trips through unfamiliar ground at night,
    returning before sunrise; stepping in the moonlight,
        on the moonlight peculiarly, that the outside
          edges of his hands may bear the weight and save the claws
        for digging. Serpentined about
          the tree, he draws
            away from danger unpugnaciously,
            with no sound but a harmless hiss; keeping

the fragile grace of the Thomas-
     of-Leighton Buzzard Westminster Abbey wrought-iron vine, or
rolls himself into a ball that has
    power to defy all effort to unroll it; strongly intailed, neat
    head for core, on neck not breaking off, with curled-in feet.
        Nevertheless he has sting-proof scales; and nest
          of rocks closed with earth from inside, which he can thus
                            darken.
        Sun and moon and day and night and man and beast
          each with a splendour
             which man in all his vileness cannot
             set aside; each with an excellence!

'Fearful yet to be feared,' the armoured
        ant-eater met by the driver-ant does not turn back, but
engulfs what he can, the flattened sword-
    edged leafpoints on the tail and artichoke set leg- and body-plates
    quivering violently when it retaliates
        and swarms on him. Compact like the furled fringed frill
          on the hat-brim of Gargallo's hollow iron head of a
        matador, he will drop and will
          then walk away
             unhurt, although if unintruded on,
             he cautiously works down the tree, helped

by his tail. The giant-pangolin-
        tail, graceful tool, as prop or hand or broom or axe, tipped like
the elephant's trunk with special skin,
    is not lost on this ant- and stone-swallowing uninjurable
    artichoke which simpletons thought a living fable
        whom the stones had nourished, whereas ants had done
          so. Pangolins are not aggressive animals; between
        dusk and day they have the not unchain-like machine-like
          form and frictionless creep of a thing
          made graceful by adversities, con-

versities. To explain grace requires
    a curious hand. If that which is at all were not forever,
why would those who graced the spires
    with animals and gathered there to rest, on cold luxurious
    low stone seats—a monk and monk and monk—between the thus
            ingenious roof-supports, have slaved to confuse
                grace with a kindly manner, time in which to pay a debt,
            the cure for sins, a graceful use
                of what are yet
                    approved stone mullions branching out across
                    the perpendiculars? A sailboat

was the first machine. Pangolins, made
    for moving quietly also, are models of exactness,
on four legs; or hind feet plantigrade,
    with certain postures of a man. Beneath sun and moon, man slaving
    to make his life more sweet, leaves half the flowers worth having,
            needing to choose wisely how to use the strength;
                a paper-maker like the wasp; a tractor of food-stuffs,
            like the ant; spidering a length
                of web from bluffs
                    above a stream; in fighting, mechanicked
                    like the pangolin; capsizing in

disheartenment. Bedizened or stark
    naked, man, the self, the being we call human, writing-
master to this world, griffons a dark
    'Like does not like like that is obnoxious'; and writes error with four
    r's. Among animals, one has a sense of humour.
            Humour saves a few steps, it saves years. Unignorant,
                modest and unemotional, and all emotion,
            he has everlasting vigour,
                power to grow,
                    though there are few creatures who can make one
                    breathe faster and make one erecter.

145

Not afraid of anything is he,
     and then goes cowering forth, tread paced to meet an obstacle
at every step. Consistent with the
   formula—warm blood, no gills, two pairs of hands and a few
                                                  hairs—that
  is a mammal; there he sits in his own habitat,
       serge-clad, strong-shod. The prey of fear, he, always
        curtailed, extinguished, thwarted by the dusk, work
                                        partly done,
      says to the alternating blaze,
       'Again the sun!
          anew each day; and new and new and new,
          that comes into and steadies my soul.'

THE EEL

The eel, the siren
of cold seas, who leaves the Baltic
to arrive at our seas,
our estuaries, our rivers,
who swims upstream in the depths, under the opposite current,
from branch to branch, then
from stem to stem as they thin out,
always further within, always more in the heart
of the rock, squeezing
through arteries of mud until one day
a light struck from the chestnut trees
ignites a quiver in deadwater sumps,
in ditches that run down
from ramparts of the Apennine to the Romagna;
the eel, whiplash, torch,
arrow of Love on earth
whom only our gulches or dried-up
Pyrenean brooks lead back
to edens of fertility;
the green soul that seeks
life where only
drought gnaws, and barrenness,
the spark that says

everything begins when everything seems
charred, a buried stump;
the brief rainbow, twin
of the one between your eyelashes
shining flawless among the sons
of man steeped in your mire, can you
not recognize in her a sister?

FRANCIS PONGE
(1899–1988)

THE OYSTER

The oyster, about as big as an average stone, looks rougher, less evenly colored, brilliantly whitish. It is a world obstinately closed. Nevertheless it can be opened: you've got to hold it in the hollow of a dish towel, use a jagged, sneaky knife, and keep trying. Inquisitive fingers get cut, nails break: it's tough work. The prying leaves its shell marked with white circles, like haloes.

Inside, you find a whole world, for eating and drinking: beneath a *firmament* (properly speaking) of mother-of-pearl, the heavens above recline on the heavens below, to form nothing more than a puddle, a viscous greenish bag that flows in and out as you smell and look at it, fringed with a blackish lace along the edges.

Sometimes, very rarely, a globule pearls in its nacreous throat, with which you immediately want to adorn yourself.

THE BUTTERFLY

When the sugar elaborated in the stems rises to the bottom of the flowers, like badly washed cups—a great effort occurs on the ground, from which butterflies suddenly take flight.

But since each caterpillar had its head blinded and left black, and its torso emaciated by the veritable explosion from which the symmetrical wings flamed,

From then on, the erratic butterfly no longer alights except by chance, or as if.

A flying matchstick, its flame is not contagious. And anyway, it arrives too late and can only ascertain that the flowers have blossomed. Never mind: acting as a lamplighter, it checks the oil supply in each. It puts on top of the flowers the atrophied rag it carries and thus avenges its long amorphous humiliation as a caterpillar at the foot of the stems.

Tiny airborne sailboat mistreated by the wind as a redundant petal, it vagabonds around the garden.

SNAILS

Unlike sneakers, which prefer dry surfaces, snails like moist earth. They move forward glued to it with their whole bodies. They carry it, they swallow it, they excrete it. It passes through them. They pass through it. It's an interpenetration in the best of taste because it is, so to speak, tone on tone—with a passive element, an active element, the passive simultaneously bathing and nourishing the active, which changes place at the same time as it eats.

(There are other things to be said about snails. To begin with, their own moisture. Their cool blood. Their extensibility.)

It might also be pointed out that you can't imagine a snail out of its shell and not moving. When it wants to rest, it returns into the depths of itself. On the other hand, its modesty obliges it to start moving as soon as it shows its nakedness and reveals its vulnerable flesh. As soon as it exposes itself, it moves on.

During dry periods, they withdraw into ditches, where the presence of their bodies apparently contributes to maintaining the moisture. There, no doubt, they find they are neighbors to other kinds of cold-blooded animals, toads, frogs. But when *they* come out, it's not at the same pace. They have more merit in going in because they have much more trouble getting out.

It might also be noted that though they like moist earth, they don't care for places where the proportion favors water, like swamps, or ponds. And certainly they prefer solid ground, provided it is rich and moist.

They are also partial to vegetables and plants with green, water-filled leaves. They eat them leaving just the veins, and cutting off the tenderest parts. They are truly the scourge of the lettuce patch.

What are they at the bottom of the ditch? Beings who like it for certain of its qualities, but who intend to climb out of it. They dwell in it as a formative but vagabond element. And furthermore, there, as well as in the broad daylight of hard paths, their shell preserves their dignity.

Certainly it is sometimes uncomfortable to carry this shell around everywhere, but they don't complain, and ultimately they're quite glad to have it. It's wonderful, wherever one is, to be able to return home and shut out intruders. This makes it well worth the trouble.

They drivel with pride at this ability, this convenience. How is it possible that I am a being so sensitive and so vulnerable, and at the same time so sheltered from the assaults of intruders, so much in possession of happiness and serenity? Thus this marvelous demeanor.

At the same time so glued to the soil, so touching and so slow, so progressive and so capable of ungluing myself from the soil to return inside myself and then after me the deluge, a kick can send me rolling anywhere. I am quite sure of putting myself back on my feet and regluing myself to the soil wherever fate has consigned me and of finding my nourishment there: the earth, the most common of foods.

What happiness, what joy then, to be a snail. But this drivel of pride is a mark that they place on everything they touch. A silvery wake follows them. And perhaps points them out to the beaks of the winged creatures for whom they are a delicacy. There's the rub, the question, to be or not to be (among the vain), the danger.

Alone, obviously the snail is very much alone. He doesn't have many friends. But he doesn't need any for his happiness. He is so well glued to nature, he enjoys it so perfectly from so close, he is the friend of the soil that he embraces with his whole body, and of the leaves, and of the sky toward which he so proudly raises his head, with its so sensitive eyeballs; nobility, slowness, wisdom, arrogance, vanity, pride.

And let's not say that in this he is like the pig. No, he doesn't have those paltry little feet, that nervous trot. That necessity, that shame of running away all in one piece. More resistant, and more stoic. More methodical, more proud, and no doubt less gluttonous,—less capricious; leaving this food in order to fall upon another, less frantic and hurried in his gluttony, less afraid of losing out on something.

Nothing is more beautiful than this way of advancing so slowly and so surely and so discreetly, at the cost of what efforts, this perfect gliding with which they honor the earth! Just like a long ship, with a silvery wake. This way of proceeding is majestic, especially if we again realize this vulnerability, these eyeballs that are so sensitive.

Is a snail's anger noticeable? Are there examples of it? Since it has no gesture, no doubt it manifests itself only by a secretion of drivel that is more flocculent and more rapid. This drivel of pride. In that case, their anger is expressed in the same way as their pride. Thus they reassure themselves and thrust themselves on the world in a richer, more silvery way.

The expression of their anger, like the expression of their pride, becomes brilliant as it dries. But it also constitutes their trail and points them out to the ravisher (the predator). Besides, it is ephemeral and lasts only till the next rain.

So it is with all those who express themselves in a wholly subjective way, unrepentant, and in traces only, with no concern for constructing and shaping their expression like a solid dwelling place, in several dimensions. More durable than themselves.

But they, no doubt, don't feel this need. They are heroes (that is, beings whose very existence is a work of art) rather than artists (that is, makers of works of art). But here I am touching on one of the main points of their lesson, which in any case is not particular to them but which they possess in common with all beings who have shells: their shell, a part of their being, is at the same time a work of art, a monument. It lasts longer than they do.

And that is the example they offer us. Saints, they make their life—their self-perfection—into a work of art. Their very secretion is produced in such a way that it shapes itself. Nothing external to them, to their necessity, to their need, is involved in their work. Nothing disproportionate—on the other hand—to their physical being. Nothing that isn't necessary, obligatory, for it.

Thus they trace man's duty for him. Great thoughts come from the heart. Perfect yourself morally and you will write beautiful poems. Morality and style combine in the ambition and desire of the sage.

But saints in what: in precisely obeying their own nature. Therefore, first know yourself. And accept yourself as you are. In accordance with your vices. In proportion to your size.

But what is the proper idea of man: speech and morality. Humanism.

THE FROG

When the rain in little slivers bounces off the drenched fields, an amphibious dwarf, a short-armed Ophelia, barely as large as a fist, sometimes springs under the poet's steps and plunges into the nearby pond.

Let her run away if she's so nervous. She has pretty legs. Her whole body is gloved in waterproof skin. Barely meat, her long muscles have an elegance neither flesh nor fish. But to escape one's fingers, the virtue of fluidity joins in her with the struggle to live. Goitrous, she pants . . . And this heart that is pounding, these wrinkled eyelids, this haggard mouth move me to let her go.

THE HORSE

Several times bigger than a man, horse has open nostrils, round eyes beneath half-closed lids, erect ears and muscular long neck.

The tallest of man's domestic animals, and truly his appointed mount.

Men, a bit lost on the elephant, are at their best on the horse, truly a throne of the right size.

We will not, I hope, abandon him?

He won't become a curiosity in a zoo, or Tiergarten?

... Already, in town, he is no more than a miserable ersatz for the car, the most miserable of all means of conveyance.

Ah! he is also—do men suspect it?—something quite different! He is *impatience* made into nostrils.

The horse's weapons are: running away, biting, bucking.

He seems to have a keen sense of smell, keen ears, and acutely sensitive eyes.

One of the finest tributes we must pay him is that we have to rig him up with blinders.

But no weapon ...

Hence the temptation to give him one. A single one. A horn.

Thus appears the unicorn.

The horse, in his great nervousness, is aerophagous.

Sensitive, to the highest degree, he tightens his jaws, holds his breath, then lets it out, making the walls of his nasal cavities vibrate loudly.

That is why the noble animal, who feeds on air and grass only, produces only straw turds and tonitruous, fragrant farts.

Fragrant tonitruisms.

What am I saying, feeds on air: he gets drunk on it. Gulps it, swallows it, snorts it.

He rushes into it, shakes his mane in it, kicks up his heels in it.

He would obviously like to leap up into it and fly.

The movement of clouds inspires him, urges him on to emulation.

He imitates them: he romps, prances.

When the lightning cracks its whip, the clouds break into a gallop, and rain tramples the ground . . .

Come out of your stall, fiery supersensitive cupboard, of polished burl!

Big beautiful antique!

Of polished ebony or mahogany.

Stroke the neck of this cupboard, and immediately there is a far-away look in its eyes.

The dust cloth at his lips, the feather-duster at his buttocks, the key in the lock of his nostrils.

His skin quivers, impatiently endures flies, his shoe hammers the ground.

He lowers his head, stretches his muzzle toward the ground and eats his fill of grass.

One needs a small bench to see what's on the upper shelf.

His skin is ticklish, I was saying . . . but his constitutional impatience is so profound that inside his body the pieces of his skeleton behave like pebbles in a torrent!

Seen from the apse, the tallest animal nave in the stable ...

Great saint! great horse! beautiful behind in the stable ...
What is this splendid courtesan's behind that greets me? mounted
on shapely legs, high heels?
Tall fowl with golden eggs, curiously clipped.
Ah! it's the smell of gold that leaps up into my nostrils!
Leather and dung mixed.
A strong-smelling omelette, from the goose with the golden eggs.
An omelette of straw, of earth: flavored with the rum of your urine,
dropping out of the crack beneath your tail ...
As if coming out of the oven, on the baker's tray, the brioches, the
rum pastries of the stable.
Great saint, your big Jewish eyes, cunning, beneath the harness ...

A kind of saint, a humble monk at his prayers, in the semi-dark-
ness.

What am I saying, a monk... No! on his excremental throne, a
pontiff! a pope—who shows first, to all comers, the splendid cour-
tesan's behind, shaped like a huge heart, on nervous legs elegantly
ending in very high-heeled shoes.

WHY THIS CLINKING OF CURB-CHAINS?
THESE DULL THUMPS IN THE STALL?
WHAT'S GOING ON IN THERE?
PONTIFF AT HIS PRAYERS?
SCHOOL KID IN DETENTION?
GREAT SAINT! GREAT HORSE, WITH YOUR BEAUTIFUL
BEHIND IN THE STABLE,
WHY, SAINTLY MONK, ARE YOU WEARING LEATHER PANTS?
—INTERRUPTED DURING HIS MASS, HE TURNED TOWARD
US HIS BIG JEWISH EYES ...

NICOLAI ZABOLOTSKY
(1903–1958)

THE FACE OF THE HORSE

Animals do not sleep. At night
They stand over the world like a stone wall.

The cow's retreating head
Rustles the straw with its smooth horns,
The rocky brow a wedge
Between age-old cheek bones,
And the mute eyes
Turning sluggishly.

There's more intelligence and beauty in the horse's face.
He hears the talk of leaves and stones.
Intent, he knows the animal's cry
And the nightingale's murmur in the copse.

And knowing all, to whom may he recount
His wonderful visions?
The night is hushed. In the dark sky
The horse stands like a knight keeping watch,
The wind plays in his light hair,
His eyes burn like two huge worlds,
And his mane lifts like the imperial purple.

And if a man should see
The horse's magical face,
He would tear out his own impotent tongue
And give it to the horse. For
This magical creature is surely worthy of it.

Then we would hear words.
Words large as apples. Thick
As honey or butter-milk.
Words which penetrate like flame
And, once within the soul, like fire in some hut,
Illuminate its wretched trappings,
Words which do not die
And which we celebrate in song.

But now the stable is empty,
The trees have dispersed,
Pinch-faced morning has swaddled the hills,
Unlocked the fields for work.
And the horse, caged within its shafts,
Dragging a covered wagon,
Gazes out of its meek eyes
Upon the enigmatic, stationary world.

Translated by Daniel Weissbort

PABLO NERUDA

(1904–1973)

SOME BEASTS

It was the twilight of the iguana.

From the rainbow-arched battlements
his tongue like a dart
plunged into the greenness,
the monastic anteater walked
through the jungle with melodious feet,
the guanaco, thin as oxygen
in the wide gray heights,
moved wearing boots of gold,
while the llama opened his guileless
eyes in the transparency
of a world filled with dew.
The monkeys braided a thread
endlessly erotic
along the shores of the dawn,
demolishing walls of pollen
and scaring off the violet flight
of the butterflies of Muzo.
It was the night of the alligators,
the night pure and pullulating
with snouts emerging from the slime,
and out of the sleepy marshes

an opaque noise of armor
returned to the earth it came from.

The jaguar touches the leaves
with his phosphorescent absence,
the puma runs on the branches
like a devouring fire
while inside him the jungle's
alcoholic eyes burn.
The badgers scratch the feet
of the river, sniff out the nest
whose throbbing delight
they'll attack with red teeth.

And in the depths of the all-powerful water,
like the circle of the earth,
lies the giant anaconda,
covered with ritual mud,
devouring and religious.

ODE TO THE BEE

Multitude of the bee!
It enters and exits
from the crimson, from the blue,
from the yellow,
from the softest
softness in the world:
it enters into
a corolla
precipitously,
for business,
it exits
with a gold suit
and a number of yellow
boots.

Perfect
from the waist,
its abdomen striped
with dark bands,
its little head
always
preoccupied
and its

wings
newly made of water:
it enters
through all the perfumed windows,
opens
the silken doors,
penetrates through the bridal chambers
of the most fragrant love,
bumps
into
a
drop
of dew
as if into a diamond
and from all the houses
that it visits
it takes out
honey,
mysterious,
rich and massive
honey, dense aroma,
liquid light that falls in thick drops,
until it returns
to its
collective
palace
and in the gothic parapets
deposits
the product
of flower and flight,
the nuptial sun, seraphic and secret!

Multitude of the bee!
Sacred

elevation
of oneness,
palpitating
academy!

Sonorous
numbers
buzz
as they work
the nectar,
quick
drops of
ambrosia
go by:
it is the siesta
of summer in the green
solitudes
of Osorno. Above,
the sun nails its spears
into the snow,
volcanoes glisten,
the land is
broad
as
the seas,
space is blue,
but
there's something
that trembles, it is
the burning
heart
of summer,
the heart of honey
multiplied,

the sonorous
bee,
the crackling
honeycomb
of flight and gold!

Bees,
pure laborers,
ogival
workers,
fine, flashing
proletarians,
perfect,
reckless militias
that in combat
attack
with suicidal sting,
buzz,
buzz over
the gifts of the earth,
family of gold,
multitude of the wind,
shake the fire
from the flowers,
the thirst from the stamens,
the sharp
thread
of smell
that unites the days,
and propagate
honey
overpassing
the moist continents, the most distant
islands of the western
sky.

Yes:
let the wax
erect green
statues,
let honey
overflow in
infinite
tongues,
and let the ocean become
a
hive,
the earth
a tower and tunic
of flowers,
and the world
a waterfall, a comet's
tail,
a ceaseless
burgeoning
of honeycombs!

ODE TO THE BLACK PANTHER

Thirty-one years ago,
I haven't forgotten,
in Singapore, rain
warm as blood
was falling
upon
ancient white walls
wormeaten
by the humidity that left in them
leprous kisses.
The dark multitude
would be lit up
suddenly by a flash
of teeth
or eyes,
with the iron sun up above
like
an implacable spear.
I wandered through the streets flooded
with *betel,* the red nuts
rising
over
beds of fragrant leaves,

and the *dorian* fruit
rotting in the muggy siesta.
Suddenly I was
in front of a gaze,
from a cage in the
middle of the street
two circles
of coldness,
two magnets,
two hostile electricities,
two eyes
that entered into mine
nailing me
to the ground
and to the leprous wall.
I saw then
the body that undulated
and was
a velvet shadow,
a flexible perfection,
pure night.
Under the black pelt,
making a subtle rainbow,
were powderlike
topaz rhomboids
or hexagons of gold,
I couldn't tell which,
that sparkled
as
the lean
presence
moved.
The panther
thinking

and palpitating
was
a
wild
queen
in a cage
in the middle of
the miserable
street.
Of the lost jungle
of deceit,
of stolen space,
of the sweet-and-sour smell of
human beings
and dusty houses
she
with mineral
eyes
only expressed
her scorn, her burning
anger,
and her eyes were
two
impenetrable
seals that
closed
till eternity
a wild door.

She walked
like fire, and, like smoke,
when she closed her eyes
she became the invisible, unencompassable night.

ODE TO THE CAT

The animals were
imperfect,
their tails were too long, their heads
too sad.
Little by little they began
to correct themselves,
they made themselves a landscape,
they acquired polka dots, grace, flight.
The cat,
only the cat
appeared complete
and proud:
was born completely finished,
walked alone and knew what he wanted.

Man wants to be a fish or a bird,
the snake wants to have wings,
the dog is a baffled lion,
the engineer wants to be a poet,
the fly studies to become a swallow,
the poet tries to imitate the fly,
but the cat
wants to be only a cat

and every cat is a cat
from his whiskers to his tail,
from his premonition to the live rat,
from the night to his golden eyes.

There is no wholeness
like his,
neither the moon
nor the flower
is put together as he is:
he is one single thing
like the sun or the topaz,
and the flexible edge of his outline
is firm and subtle like
the line of a ship's prow.
His yellow eyes
leave a single
slot
to spill out the coins of the night.

O little
emperor without an orb,
conquistador without a country,
tiny living-room tiger, nuptial
sultan of the sky
of erotic rooftops,
you reclaim
the wind of love
in the open air
when you walk by
and put
four delicate feet
on the ground,
sniffing,

mistrustful of
everything on earth,
because everything
is unclean
for the cat's immaculate foot.

O fierce independent
of the house, proud
remnant of the night,
lazy, gymnastic
and detached,
O master of profundity,
secret police
of the neighborhoods,
emblem
of a
disappeared velvet,
surely there is no
enigma
in your behavior,
perhaps you aren't a mystery,
everyone knows you, you belong
to the least mysterious neighbor,
perhaps everyone believes it,
believes he is the master,
the proprietor, the uncle,
the companion,
the colleague,
the disciple or friend
of his cat.

Not me.
I don't buy it.
I don't know who the cat is.

Everything else I know, life
and its archipelago,
the sea and the incalculable city,
botany,
the pistil with its deviations,
the plus and the minus of mathematics,
the volcanic funnels of the world,
the unreal husk of the crocodile,
the hidden kindness of the fireman,
the blue atavism of the priest,
but I can't decipher a cat.
My mind slides in his indifference,
in the golden numbers of his eyes.

ODE TO THE HUMMINGBIRD

To the flower-sipper,
flying
spark of water,
incandescent drop
of American
fire,
brilliant
epitome
of the jungle,
rainbow
of celestial
precision:
to the
hummingbird,
an arc,
a
golden
thread,
a blaze
of green!

O
tiny

animated
lightningflash,
as
your
structure
of pollen
hovers
in the air,
feather
or live coal,
I ask you,
what are you, where
is your origin?
Perhaps in the blind age
of the flood,
in the mire
of fertility,
when
the rose
congealed into a fist of coal
and metals signed up,
each one in
its secret
cubicle,
perhaps then
from the wounded
reptile
one fragment whirled out,
one atom
of gold,
the final
cosmic sliver, one
drop
of earthly fire,

and it flew
dangling your beauty,
your iridescent
and quick sapphire.

You sleep
in a walnut,
fit into a
minuscule corolla,
arrow,
invention,
coat-of-arms,
vibration
of honey, ray of pollen,
you are
so valiant
that the falcon
with his black plumage
doesn't frighten you:
you turn
like light in light,
air in air,
and fly into
the moist coffer of
a quivering flower
without fear
that its nuptial honey will behead you.
From scarlet to powdered gold,
to blazing yellow,
to the rare
ashen emerald,
to the orange-and-black velvet
of your shimmering corselet,
out to the tip

that like
an amber thorn
begins you,
small, superlative being,
you are a miracle,
and you blaze
from
warm California
to the whistling
of the bitter winds of Patagonia.
You are seed
of the sun,
feathered
flame,
minuscule
streaming
banner,
petal of silenced races,
syllable
of buried blood,
plume
of the ancient
submerged
heart.

PABLO NERUDA

ODE TO THE ROOSTER

I saw a rooster
with Castilian
plumage:
from black and white cloth
his shirt
had been cut,
and his knee-breeches,
and the arched feathers
of his tail.
His feet, sheathed
in yellow boots,
revealed
the glitter of his defiant
spurs,
and on top
the lordly
head,
crowned
with blood,
maintained
that demeanor:
a statue
of pride.

Never
on
earth
had I seen such confidence,
such valor:
it was
as if fire
had hoisted
the final precision
of its beauty:
two dark
flashes
of jet
were
the disdainful eyes
of the rooster
who walked as
if he were dancing,
almost without touching the ground.

But the moment
his eyes saw
a grain
of corn or a crumb
of bread,
he lifted it in his beak
as a jeweler's
delicate fingers hold up
a diamond,
then
with a guttural oration he called
his hens
and from on high let the food
fall.

Never have I seen a president
with gold braid and stars
adorned
like this
rooster
parceling out
wheat,
nor have I seen
a tenor
unapproachable
as this pure
protagonist of gold
who from
the central
throne of his universe
protected the women
of his tribe
keeping nothing in his mouth
but pride,
looking in all directions,
searching for
the food
of the earth
only
for his insatiable
family,
walking toward
the sun, toward the slopes,
toward another grain
of wheat.

Your dignity like a tower's,
like a benign
warrior's,
your hymn

lifted
to the heights,
your quick
love, rapture
of feathered shadows,
I celebrate,
black and
white
rooster,
strutting
epitome
of virile honor,
father
of the fragile egg, paladin
of the dawn,
bird of pride,
bird without a nest,
who bestows his sacrifice
upon mankind
without compromising
his lineage,
or ruining his song.

Your nobility
doesn't need flight,
field marshal of love
and meteor
devoted
to so many excellences
that if this
ode
falls
into the coop
you will peck it with supreme aloofness
and parcel it out to your hens.

ODE TO THE SEAGULL

To the seagull
above
the pine woods
of the coast,
on the wind
the sibilant
syllable of my ode.

Sail along
in my verse,
shining boat,
banner with two wings,
body of silver,
lift up
your emblem across
the shirt
of the cold firmament,
O sky-sailor,
smooth
serenade of flight,
arrow of snow, calm
ship in the transparent storm,
you raise your equilibrium

while
the hoarse wind sweeps
the meadows of the sky.

After your long journey,
feathered magnolia,
triangle whom the air
holds up into the heights,
slowly you come back
to your form
closing
your silver garment,
ovaling your brilliant treasure,
becoming once again
a white bud of flight,
round
seed,
egg of beauty.

Another poet
at this point
would end
his triumphant ode.
I cannot
allow myself
just
the white luxury
of the useless foam.
Forgive me,
seagull,
I am
a poet
of reality,
a photographer of the sky.

You eat,
eat,
eat,
there's
nothing you don't devour,
over the water of the bay
you bark
like a poor man's dog,
you run
after the last
scrap of fish guts,
you peck
at your white sisters,
you steal
the despicable prize,
the crumbling heap
of oceanic garbage,
you scout for
rotten
tomatoes,
the discarded
refuse of the cove.
But
you transform
all of it
into pure wing,
white geometry,
the ecstatic line of your flight.

That's why,
snowy anchor,
sky-sailor,
I celebrate you as a whole:
with your overwhelming voraciousness,

with your screech in the rain
or your rest
like a snowflake detached
from the storm,
with your peace or your flight,
seagull,
I consecrate to you
my earthly words,
a clumsy attempt at flight,
to see
if you will scatter
your birdseed in my ode.

ODE TO THE YELLOW BIRD

I buried you in the garden:
a grave
tiny
as an open hand,
southern
earth,
cold earth
fell covering
your plumage,
the yellow rays,
the black lightnings
of your snuffed-out body.
From Matto Grosso,
from fertile Goiania
they sent you
locked up.
You couldn't bear it.
You left.
In the cage
with your small
feet stiff,
as though clutching
an invisible branch,

dead,
a poor clump
of extinguished feathers,
far away
from your native fires,
from the maternal
thicket,
in cold earth,
far away.
Bird
most pure,
I knew you alive,
electric,
excited,
murmurous,
your body was
a fragrant
arrow,
on my arm and shoulders
you walked
independent, untamed,
black as black stone
and pollen-yellow.
O wild
beauty,
the proud determination
of your steps,
in your eyes
the spark
of defiance, but
as
a flower is defiant,
with the wholeness
of an earthly integrity, filled up

like a bunch of grapes, restless
as a discoverer,
safe
in your frail arrogance.

I did wrong: to the autumn
that is beginning
in my country,
to the leaves
that fade now
and fall,
to the galvanic wind of the south,
to the hard trees, to the leaves
that you didn't know,
I brought you,
I made your pride travel
to a different, ashen sun
far from your own
that burns
like a scarlet zither,
and when
at the metallic hangar
your cage
landed,
already you had lost
the majesty of the wind,
already you had been stripped
of the zenith's light that had covered you,
already you were
a feather of death,
and then,
in my house,
your final look was
into my face, the reproach

of your untamable gaze.
Later,
with wings closed,
you went back
to your sky,
to the spacious heart,
to the green fire,
to the ignited earth,
to the slopes,
to the trailing vines,
to the fruits,
to the air, to the stars,
to the secret sound
of unknown springs,
to the moisture
of fecundations in the jungle,
you went back
to your origin,
to the yellow brilliance,
to the dark breast,
to the earth and sky of your home.

HORSES

From the window I saw the horses.

I was in Berlin, in winter. The light
was without light, the sky without sky.

The air white like wet bread.

And from my window a vacant arena,
bitten by the teeth of winter.

Suddenly, led by a man,
ten horses stepped out into the mist.

Hardly had they surged forth, like flame,
than to my eyes they filled the whole world,
empty till then. Perfect, ablaze,
they were like ten gods with wide pure hoofs,
with manes like a dream of salt.

Their rumps were worlds and oranges.

Their color was honey, amber, fire.

Their necks were towers
cut from the stone of pride,

and behind their transparent eyes
energy raged, like a prisoner.

And there, in the silence, in the middle
of the day, of the dark, slovenly winter,
the intense horses were blood
and rhythm, the animating treasure of life.

I looked, I looked and was reborn: without knowing it,
there, was the fountain, the dance of gold, the sky,
the fire that revived in beauty.

I have forgotten that dark Berlin winter.

I will not forget the light of the horses.

CATS' DREAM

How nicely a cat sleeps,
sleeps with its paws and its gravity,
sleeps with its cruel claws,
and with its sanguinary blood,
sleeps with all the rings
which, like burnt circles,
compose the geology
of a tail the color of sand.

I would like to sleep like a cat
with all the hairs of time,
with the tongue of flint,
with the dry sex of fire
and after speaking with no one
to stretch myself over the whole world,
over the roof-tiles and the ground
intensely determined
to go hunting the rats of dream.

I have seen how the cat as it slept
would undulate: the night
flowed in it like dark water,
and at times it was going to fall,

maybe it was going to plunge
into the naked snowdrifts,
or it grew so much as it slept
like a tiger's great-grandfather
that it overleapt in the darkness
roofs, clouds, and volcanoes.

Sleep, sleep, nocturnal cat,
with your ceremonies of a bishop
and your moustache of stone:
supervise all our dreams,
manage the darkness
of our slumbered powers
with your sanguinary heart
and the long collar of your tail.

BESTIARY

If only I could speak with birds,
with oysters and with small lizards,
with the foxes of Selva Oscura,
with representative penguins,
if the sheep would listen to me,
the languorous, wooly dogs,
the huge carriage-horses, if only
I could talk things over with the cats,
if the chickens could understand me!

I have never felt the urge to speak
with aristocratic animals:
I am not at all interested
in the world view of the wasps
or the opinions of thoroughbred horses:
so what, if they go on flying
or winning ribbons at the track!
I want to speak with the flies,
with the bitch who has just given birth,
to have a long chat with the snakes.

When my feet were able to walk
through triple nights, now past,

I followed the nocturnal dogs,
those squalid, incessant travelers
who trot around town in silence
in their great rush to nowhere,
and I followed them for hours,
they were quite suspicious of me,
those poor foolish dogs,
they lost the opportunity
of telling me their sorrows,
of running with grief and a tail
through the avenues of the ghosts.

I was always very curious
about the erotic rabbit:
who provokes it and whispers
into its genital ears?
It never stops procreating
and takes no notice of Saint Francis,
doesn't listen to nonsense:
the rabbit keeps on humping
with its inexhaustible mechanism.
I'd like to speak with the rabbit,
I love its sexy customs.

The spiders have always been slandered
in the idiotic pages
of exasperating simplifiers
who take the fly's point of view,
who describe them as devouring,
carnal, unfaithful, lascivious.
For me, that reputation
discredits just those who concocted it:
the spider is an engineer,
a divine maker of watches,

for one fly more or less
let the imbeciles detest them,
I want to have a talk with the spider,
I want her to weave me a star.

The fleas interest me so much
that I let them bite me for hours,
they are perfect, ancient, Sanskritic,
they are inexorable machines.
They don't bite in order to eat,
they bite in order to jump,
they're the globe's champion highjumpers,
the smoothest and most profound
acrobats in the circus:
let them gallop across my skin,
let them reveal their emotions
and amuse themselves with my blood,
just let me be introduced to them,
I want to know them from up close,
I want to know what I can count on.

With the ruminants I haven't been able
to achieve an intimate friendship:
I myself am a ruminant, I can't see
why they don't understand me.
I'll have to study this theme
grazing with cows and oxen,
making plans with the bulls.
Somehow I will come to know
so many intestinal things
hidden inside my body
like the most clandestine passions.

What do pigs think of the dawn?
They don't sing but they carry it

with their large pink bodies,
with their little hard hooves.

The pigs carry the dawn.

The birds eat up the night.

And in the morning the world
is deserted: the spiders sleep,
the humans, the dogs, the wind sleeps,
the pigs grunt, and day breaks.

I want to have a talk with the pigs.

Sweet, loud, harsh-voiced frogs,
I have always wanted to be
a frog, I have loved the pools
and the leaves, thin as filaments,
the green world of the watercress
with the frogs, queens of the sky.
The serenade of the frog
rises in my dream and excites it,
rises like a climbing vine
to the balconies of my childhood,
to the budding nipples of my cousin,
to the astronomic jasmine
of the black night of the South,
and now so much time has passed,
don't ask me about the sky:
I feel that I haven't yet learned
the harsh-voiced idiom of the frogs.

If this is so, how am I a poet?
What do I know of the multiplied
geography of the night?

In this world that rushes and grows calm
I want more communications,
other languages, other signs,
to be intimate with this world.

Everyone has remained content
with the sinister presentations
of rapid capitalists
and systematic women.
I want to speak with many things
and I won't leave this planet
without knowing what I came to find,
without resolving this matter,
and people are not enough,
I have to go much farther
and I have to get much closer.

And so, gentlemen, I'm going
to have a talk with a horse,
let the poetess excuse me
and let the professor pardon me,
all week I'll be busy,
I have to constantly listen.

What was the name of that cat?

BIRD

It fell from one bird to another,
everything the day brought,
the day went from flute to flute,
it went dressed in greenness,
with flights that opened a tunnel,
and inside was the wind
by which the birds opened
the air, dense and blue:
through it entered the night.

When I came home from so many journeys,
I stayed suspended and green
between the sun and geography:
I saw how wings worked,
how fragrance is transmitted
by a feathered telegraph,
and from above I saw the road,
the springs, the roof tiles,
the fishermen fishing,
the trousers of the foam,
everything from my green sky.
I had no more alphabet
than the journeying of the swallows,

the pure and tiny water
of the small, fiery bird
that dances rising from the pollen.

THEODORE ROETHKE

(1908–1963)

THE MEADOW MOUSE

I

In a shoe box stuffed in an old nylon stocking
Sleeps the baby mouse I found in the meadow,
Where he trembled and shook beneath a stick
Till I caught him up by the tail and brought him in,
Cradled in my hand,
A little quaker, the whole body of him trembling,
His absurd whiskers sticking out like a cartoon-mouse,
His feet like small leaves,
Little lizard-feet,
Whitish and spread wide when he tried to struggle away,
Wriggling like a minuscule puppy.

Now he's eaten his three kinds of cheese and drunk from his
      bottle-cap watering-trough—
So much he just lies in one corner,
His tail curled under him, his belly big
As his head; his bat-like ears
Twitching, tilting toward the least sound.

Do I imagine he no longer trembles
When I come close to him?
He seems no longer to tremble.

II

But this morning the shoe-box house on the back porch is empty.
Where has he gone, my meadow mouse,
My thumb of a child that nuzzled in my palm?—
To run under the hawk's wing,
Under the eye of the great owl watching from the elm-tree,
To live by courtesy of the shrike, the snake, the tom-cat.

I think of the nestling fallen into the deep grass,
The turtle gasping in the dusty rubble of the highway,
The paralytic stunned in the tub, and the water rising,—
All things innocent, hapless, forsaken.

ELIZABETH BISHOP
(1911–1979)

THE FISH

I caught a tremendous fish
and held him beside the boat
half out of water, with my hook
fast in a corner of his mouth.
He didn't fight.
He hadn't fought at all.
He hung a grunting weight,
battered and venerable
and homely. Here and there
his brown skin hung in strips
like ancient wallpaper,
and its pattern of darker brown
was like wallpaper:
shapes like full-blown roses
stained and lost through age.
He was speckled with barnacles,
fine rosettes of lime,
and infested
with tiny white sea-lice,
and underneath two or three
rags of green weed hung down.
While his gills were breathing in
the terrible oxygen

—the frightening gills,
fresh and crisp with blood,
that can cut so badly—
I thought of the coarse white flesh
packed in like feathers,
the big bones and the little bones,
the dramatic reds and blacks
of his shiny entrails,
and the pink swim-bladder
like a big peony.
I looked into his eyes
which were far larger than mine
but shallower, and yellowed,
the irises backed and packed
with tarnished tinfoil
seen through the lenses
of old scratched isinglass.
They shifted a little, but not
to return my stare.
—It was more like the tipping
of an object toward the light.
I admired his sullen face,
the mechanism of his jaw,
and then I saw
that from his lower lip
—if you could call it a lip—
grim, wet, and weaponlike,
hung five old pieces of fish-line,
or four and a wire leader
with the swivel still attached,
with all their five big hooks
grown firmly in his mouth.
A green line, frayed at the end
where he broke it, two heavier lines,

and a fine black thread
still crimped from the strain and snap
when it broke and he got away.
Like medals with their ribbons
frayed and wavering,
a five-haired beard of wisdom
trailing from his aching jaw.
I stared and stared
and victory filled up
the little rented boat,
from the pool of bilge
where oil had spread a rainbow
around the rusted engine
to the bailer rusted orange,
the sun-cracked thwarts,
the oarlocks on their strings,
the gunnels—until everything
was rainbow, rainbow, rainbow!
And I let the fish go.

SANDPIPER

The roaring alongside he takes for granted,
and that every so often the world is bound to shake.
He runs, he runs to the south, finical, awkward,
in a state of controlled panic, a student of Blake.

The beach hisses like fat. On his left, a sheet
of interrupting water comes and goes
and glazes over his dark and brittle feet.
He runs, he runs straight through it, watching his toes.

—Watching, rather, the spaces of sand between them,
where (no detail too small) the Atlantic drains
rapidly backwards and downwards. As he runs,
he stares at the dragging grains.

The world is a mist. And then the world is
minute and vast and clear. The tide
is higher or lower. He couldn't tell you which.
His beak is focussed; he is preoccupied,

looking for something, something, something.
Poor bird, he is obsessed!
The millions of grains are black, white, tan, and gray,
mixed with quartz grains, rose and amethyst.

RAINY SEASON; SUB-TROPICS

Giant Toad

I am too big, too big by far. Pity me.

My eyes bulge and hurt. They are my one great beauty, even so. They see too much, above, below, and yet there is not much to see. The rain has stopped. The mist is gathering on my skin in drops. The drops run down my back, run from the corners of my downturned mouth, run down my sides and drip beneath my belly. Perhaps the droplets on my mottled hide are pretty, like dewdrops, silver on a moldering leaf? They chill me through and through. I feel my colors changing now, my pigments gradually shudder and shift over.

Now I shall get beneath that overhanging ledge. Slowly. Hop. Two or three times more, silently. That was too far. I'm standing up. The lichen's gray, and rough to my front feet. Get down. Turn facing out, it's safer. Don't breathe until the snail gets by. But we go travelling the same weathers.

Swallow the air and mouthfuls of cold mist. Give voice, just once. O how it echoed from the rock! What a profound, angelic bell I rang!

I live, I breathe, by swallowing. Once, some naughty children picked me up, me and two brothers. They set us down again somewhere and in our mouths they put lit cigarettes. We could not help but smoke them, to the end. I thought it was the death of me, but when I was entirely filled with smoke, when my slack mouth was burning, and all my tripes were hot and dry, they let us go. But I was sick for days.

I have big shoulders, like a boxer. They are not muscle, however, and their color is dark. They are my sacs of poison, the almost unused poison that I bear, my burden and my great responsibility. Big wings of poison, folded on my back. Beware, I am an angel in disguise; my wings are evil, but not deadly. If I will it, the poison could break through, blue-black, and dangerous to all. Blue-black fumes would rise upon the air. Beware, you frivolous crab.

Strayed Crab

This is not my home. How did I get so far from water? It must be over that way somewhere.

I am the color of wine, of *tinta*. The inside of my powerful right claw is saffron-yellow. See, I see it now; I wave it like a flag. I am dapper and elegant; I move with great precision, cleverly managing all my smaller yellow claws. I believe in the oblique, the indirect approach, and I keep my feelings to myself.

But on this strange, smooth surface I am making too much noise. I wasn't meant for this. If I maneuver a bit and keep a sharp lookout, I shall find my pool again. Watch out for my right claw, all passersby! This place is too hard. The rain has stopped, and it is damp, but still not wet enough to please me.

My eyes are good, though small; my shell is tough and tight. In my own pool are many small gray fish. I see right through them. Only their large eyes are opaque, and twitch at me. They are hard to catch, but I, I catch them quickly in my arms and eat them up.

What is that big soft monster, like a yellow cloud, stifling and warm? What is it doing? It pats my back. Out, claw. There, I have frightened it away. It's sitting down, pretending nothing's happened. I'll skirt it. It's still pretending not to see me. Out of my way, O monster. I own a pool, all the little fish swim in it, and all the skittering waterbugs that smell like rotten apples.

Cheer up, O grievous snail. I tap your shell, encouragingly, not that you will ever know about it.

And I want nothing to do with you, either, sulking toad. Imagine, at least four times my size and yet so vulnerable . . . I could open your belly with my claw. You glare and bulge, a watchdog near my pool; you make a loud and hollow noise. I do not care for such stupidity. I admire compression, lightness, and agility, all rare in this loose world.

Giant Snail

The rain has stopped. The waterfall will roar like that all night. I have come out to take a walk and feed. My body—foot, that is—is wet and cold and covered with sharp gravel. It is white, the size of a dinner plate. I have set myself a goal, a certain rock, but it may well be dawn before I get there. Although I move ghostlike and my floating edges barely graze the ground, I am heavy, heavy, heavy. My white muscles are already tired. I give the impression of mysterious ease, but it is only with the greatest effort of my will that I can rise above the smallest stones and sticks. And I must not let myself be distracted by those rough spears of grass. Don't touch them. Draw back. Withdrawal is always best.

The rain has stopped. The waterfall makes such a noise! (And what if I fall over it?) The mountains of black rock give off clouds of steam! Shiny streamers are hanging down their sides. When this occurs, we have a saying that the Snail Gods have come down in haste. *I* could never descend such steep escarpments, much less dream of climbing them.

That toad was too big, too, like me. His eyes beseeched my love. Our proportions horrify our neighbors.

Rest a minute; relax. Flattened to the ground, my body is like a pallid, decomposing leaf. What's that tapping on my shell? Nothing. Let's go on.

My sides move in rhythmic waves, just off the ground, from front to back, the wake of a ship, wax-white water, or a slowly melting floe. I am cold, cold, cold as ice. My blind, white bull's head was a Cretan scare-head; degenerate, my four horns that can't attack. The sides of my mouth are now my hands. They press the earth and suck it hard. Ah, but I know my shell is beautiful, and high, and glazed, and shining. I know it well, although I have not seen it. Its curled white lip is of the finest enamel. Inside, it is as smooth as silk, and I, I fill it to perfection.

My wide wake shines, now it is growing dark. I leave a lovely opalescent ribbon: I know this.

But O! I am too big. I feel it. Pity me.

If and when I reach the rock, I shall go into a certain crack there for the night. The waterfall below will vibrate through my shell and body all night long. In that steady pulsing I can rest. All night I shall be like a sleeping ear.

FIVE FLIGHTS UP

Still dark.
The unknown bird sits on his usual branch.
The little dog next door barks in his sleep
inquiringly, just once.
Perhaps in his sleep, too, the bird inquires
once or twice, quavering.
Questions—if that is what they are—
answered directly, simply,
by day itself.

Enormous morning, ponderous, meticulous;
gray light streaking each bare branch,
each single twig, along one side,
making another tree, of glassy veins . . .
The bird still sits there. Now he seems to yawn.

The little black dog runs in his yard.
His owner's voice arises, stern,
"You ought to be ashamed!"
What has he done?
He bounces cheerfully up and down;
he rushes in circles in the fallen leaves.

Obviously, he has no sense of shame.
He and the bird know everything is answered,
all taken care of,
no need to ask again.
—Yesterday brought to today so lightly!
(A yesterday I find almost impossible to lift.)

RANDALL JARRELL

(1914–1965)

THE BIRD OF NIGHT

A shadow is floating through the moonlight.
Its wings don't make a sound.
Its claws are long, its beak is bright.
Its eyes try all the corners of the night.

It calls and calls: all the air swells and heaves
And washes up and down like water.
The ear that listens to the owl believes
In death. The bat beneath the eaves,

The mouse beside the stone are still as death.
The owl's air washes them like water.
The owl goes back and forth inside the night,
And the night holds its breath.

BATS

A bat is born
Naked and blind and pale.
His mother makes a pocket of her tail
And catches him. He clings to her long fur
By his thumbs and toes and teeth.
And then the mother dances through the night
Doubling and looping, soaring, somersaulting—
Her baby hangs on underneath.
All night, in happiness, she hunts and flies.
Her high sharp cries
Like shining needlepoints of sound
Go out into the night and, echoing back,
Tell her what they have touched.
She hears how far it is, how big it is,
Which way it's going:
She lives by hearing.
The mother eats the moths and gnats she catches
In full flight; in full flight
The mother drinks the water of the pond
She skims across. Her baby hangs on tight.
Her baby drinks the milk she makes him
In moonlight or starlight, in mid-air.
Their single shadow, printed on the moon

Or fluttering across the stars,
Whirls on all night; at daybreak
The tired mother flaps home to her rafter.
The others all are there.
They hang themselves up by their toes,
They wrap themselves in their brown wings.
Bunched upside-down, they sleep in air.
Their sharp ears, their sharp teeth, their quick sharp faces
Are dull and slow and mild.
All the bright day, as the mother sleeps,
She folds her wings about her sleeping child.

FIRST SIGHT

Lambs that learn to walk in snow
When their bleating clouds the air
Meet a vast unwelcome, know
Nothing but a sunless glare.
Newly stumbling to and fro
All they find, outside the fold,
Is a wretched width of cold.

As they wait beside the ewe,
Her fleeces wetly caked, there lies
Hidden round them, waiting too,
Earth's immeasurable surprise.
They could not grasp it if they knew,
What so soon will wake and grow
Utterly unlike the snow.

JAMES WRIGHT
(1927–1980)

A BLESSING

Just off the highway to Rochester, Minnesota,
Twilight bounds softly forth on the grass.
And the eyes of those two Indian ponies
Darken with kindness.
They have come gladly out of the willows
To welcome my friend and me.
We step over the barbed wire into the pasture
Where they have been grazing all day, alone.
They ripple tensely, they can hardly contain their happiness
That we have come.
They bow shyly as wet swans. They love each other.
There is no loneliness like theirs.
At home once more,
They begin munching the young tufts of spring in the darkness.
I would like to hold the slenderer one in my arms,
For she has walked over to me
And nuzzled my left hand.
She is black and white,
Her mane falls wild on her forehead,
And the light breeze moves me to caress her long ear
That is delicate as the skin over a girl's wrist.
Suddenly I realize
That if I stepped out of my body I would break
Into blossom.

THE TURTLE OVERNIGHT

I remember him last twilight in his comeliness. When it began to rain, he appeared in his accustomed place and emerged from his shell as far as he could reach—feet, legs, tail, head. He seemed to enjoy the rain, the sweet-tasting rain that blew all the way across lake water to him from the mountains, the Alto Adige. It was as near as I've ever come to seeing a turtle take a pleasant bath in his natural altogether. All the legendary faces of broken old age disappeared from my mind, the thickened muscles under the chins, the nostrils brutal with hatred, the murdering eyes. He filled my mind with a sweet-tasting mountain rain, his youthfulness, his modesty as he washed himself all alone, his religious face.

For a long time now this morning, I have been sitting at this window and watching the grass below me. A moment ago there was no one there. But now his brindle shell sighs slowly up and down in the midst of the green sunlight. A black watchdog snuffles asleep just beyond him, but I trust that neither is afraid of the other. I can see him lifting his face. It is a raising of the eyebrows toward the light, an almost imperceptible turning of the chin, an ancient pleasure, an eagerness.

Along his throat there are small folds, dark yellow as pollen shaken across a field of camomilla. The lines on his face suggest only a relaxation, a delicacy in the understanding of the grass, like the careful tenderness I saw once on the face of a hobo in Ohio as he waved greeting to an empty wheat field from the flatcar of a freight train.

But now the train is gone, and the turtle has left his circle of empty grass. I look a long time where he was, and I can't find a footprint in the empty grass. So much air left, so much sunlight, and still he is gone.

A DARK MOOR BIRD

A dark moor bird has come down from the mountains
To test the season.
He flies low across the Adige and seines
The brilliant web of his shadow behind him.
Slender and sure,
His wings give him the nobility
Of a small swan.
But his voice
Ruins it, he has seen me and he can't
Shut up about it.
He sounds
Like a plump chicken nagging a raccoon
Who is trying to get out of the henhouse
With a little dignity.

I wonder why the beautiful moor bird
Won't leave me alone.
All I am doing is standing here,
Turning to stone,
Believing he will build a strong nest
Along the Adige, hoping
He will never die.

BUTTERFLY FISH

Not five seconds ago, I saw him flutter so quick
And tremble with so mighty a trembling,
He was gone.
He left this clear depth of coral
Between his moments.
Now, he is here, back,
Slow and lazy.
He knows already he is so alive he can leave me alone,
Peering down, holding his empty mountains,
Happy in easy luxury, he grazes up his tall corals,
Slim as a stallion, serene on his far-off hillside,
His other world where I cannot see
His secret face.

A MOUSE TAKING A NAP

I look all alike to him, one blur of nervous mountains after another. I doubt if he loses any sleep in brooding and puzzling out why it is I don't like him. The huge slopes and valleys, golden as wild mustard flowers in midsummer, that he leaves lying open and naked down the sides of a Gorgonzola, seem to him only a discovery, one of the lonely paradises: nothing like the gray wound of a slag heap, nothing like the streams of copperous water that ooze out of the mine-mouths in southern Ohio. I wonder what it seems to him, his moment that he has now, alone with his own sunlight in this locked house, where all the cats are gone for a little while, hunting somebody else for a little while.

LIGHTNING BUGS ASLEEP IN THE AFTERNOON

These long-suffering and affectionate shadows,
These fluttering jewels, are trying to get
Some sleep in a dry shade beneath the cement
Joists of the railroad trestle.

I did not climb up here to find them.
It was only my ordinary solitude
I was following up here this afternoon.
Last evening I sat here with a girl.

It was a dangerous place to be a girl
And young. But she simply folded her silent
Skirt over bare knees, printed with the flowered cotton
Of a meal sack her mother had stitched for her.

Neither of us said anything to speak of.
These affectionate, these fluttering bodies
Signaled to one another under the bridge
While the B&O 40-and-8's rattled away.

Now ordinary and alone in the afternoon,
I find this little circle of insects
Common as soot, clustering on dim stone,
Together with their warm secrets.

I think I am going to leave them folded
And sleeping in their slight gray wings.
I think I am going to climb back down
And open my eyes and shine.

All translations and adaptations in this book are mine unless otherwise indicated.

My version of the Akhenaton "Hymn to the Sun" is adapted from the translations by John A. Wilson in *Ancient Near Eastern Texts Relating to the Old Testament,* Third Edition, edited by James B. Pritchard (Princeton, 1969), and of Fred Gladstone Bratton in *The First Heretic: The Life and Times of Ikhnaton the King* (New York, 1961). My versions of Issa are adapted from the translations of Lucien Stryk and Takashi Ikemoto, and of David G. Lanoue. In the course of checking my versions of Ponge, I borrowed a number of phrases from Beth Archer's translations in *The Voice of Things* (New York, 1972).

ACKNOWLEDGMENTS

I would like to express my gratitude to Robert Hass for translating some of the Basho and Issa haiku on the wing, at my request; to Richard Wilbur for pointing me to four poems which I hadn't read with my ears open; to Richard Grossinger for enabling this book to walk the bodhisattva path; to Anastasia McGhee for her creative co-imagination; to Paula Morrison for her lovely design; to Marianne Dresser for her skill and patience with a difficult job of copyediting; to the staff at Frog, Ltd. for their long-distance tiger's roar; and to Michael Katz, my agent, for his excellent advice.

And, as always, to Vicki.